Creed
to
Deed

Creed
to
Deed

Living an Apostolic Faith
in a Culture of Conformity

Jonathan
Lawson

invite
PRESS

Plano, Texas

Table of Contents

The Apostles' Creed

I believe in God the Father Almighty,
Creator of Heaven and Earth.

And in Jesus Christ, His Only Son, our Lord,
who was conceived by the Holy Spirit,
Born of the Virgin Mary,
Suffered under Pontius Pilate,
was crucified, died, and was buried.
He descended to the dead.
On the third day, he rose from the dead.
He ascended into Heaven,
and sits at the right hand of God the Father Almighty.
From there he shall come to judge the living and the dead.

I believe in the Holy Spirit,
the holy catholic church,
the communion of saints,
the forgiveness of sins,
the resurrection of the body,
and the life everlasting. Amen.

Preface

Some in the church today believe that we are seeing a world of increasing secularization, a world abandoning faith. But in reality, a resurgence of faith and spirituality in our society is exploding right before our eyes. Far from abandoning faith, people are looking for it somewhere other than the Christian church. The truth is, spirituality is big business these days, and we are seeing not only the resurgence of modern paganism and Eastern religions but an increase in religious devotion to scientific assertions.

The good news is that more than at any time in the last 200 years, people are recognizing their need for more profound answers than a materialistic view of reality can offer. If we believe that the Christian faith is the one true revelation of God and the meaning of all creation, then we should celebrate the opportunity for open conversations with which we are being presented. But are we prepared? Can we offer those seeking answers the "faith once delivered to the saints"? (Jude 1:3)

Barna Research found in 2009 that only 19 percent of "born again Christians" in America held a biblical worldview. *Biblical worldview* is defined as[1]:

---

1. *Born Again Christian* is defined as "having made a personal commitment to Jesus Christ that is important in their life today and that they are certain that they will go to heaven after they die only because they confessed their sins and accepted Christ as their savior" from "Changes in Worldview Among Christians over the Past 13 Years," Barna, March 9, 2009, https://www.barna.com/research/barna-survey-examines-changes-in-worldview-among-christians-over-the-past-13-years/

- There is an absolute moral truth.
- The Bible is totally accurate in all the principles it teaches.
- Satan is considered to be a real being or force, not merely symbolic.
- A person cannot earn their way into heaven by trying to be good or do good works.
- Jesus Christ lived a sinless life on Earth.
- God is the all-knowing, all-powerful creator of the world who still rules the universe today.

This number slipped further to only 17 percent in 2017.[2] Notable among these findings are that:

- 61 percent of practicing Christians agree with ideas rooted in New Spiritualism.
- 54 percent agree with postmodernist views.
- 36 percent accept ideas associated with Marxism.
- 29 percent believe ideas based on secularism.

If we, the Church, are going to share the Christian faith with a hungry and searching world, we need first to be sure we indeed know what constitutes that faith. Although "experiential religion" served a much-needed function in bringing spiritual revival to both America and the rest of the world over the last two centuries, it has also resulted in the loss of sound catechism of Christian believers in the faith. *Catechism* is even a foreign and strange word to most of us. Still, it captures the appropriate mix of teaching and training necessary to provide the knowledge base required for proper spiritual formation through more experiential tactics. This is not a bid to return to merely an intellectual approach to Christianity but to equip believers with the ability to correctly interpret their subjective

---

2. "Competing Worldviews Influence Today's Christians," *Barna*, May 9, 2017, https://www.barna.com/research/competing-worldviews-influence-todays-christians/

experiences in the light of objective truth, which resides outside of themselves.

In seeking to re-establish the core of Christian belief for ourselves, our families, and our churches, we would do well to look to those who stood closest to the origins of this faith and stood firm in the face of its greatest persecutions. The Apostles' Creed is an ancient confession affirmed by the earliest practices and councils of an undivided church. Its name and provenance are derived from those sent out by Christ himself, who walked alongside him during his earthly ministry and witnessed his Resurrection in the forty days leading up to his Ascension into Heaven. It was used by the early church as a Baptismal Confession for those who had completed three years of catechism and discipleship in the faith and forty days of fasting and prayer before the Easter Vigil. It represents the summarization of the necessary elements of faith unto salvation and can be said to have been believed by all true Christians, through all times, everywhere.

While particular doctrines not addressed within the Apostles' Creed may be within the bounds of orthodoxy, it represents the core tenets of Christianity. It is arranged appropriately around the confession of the Holy Trinity. It makes statements about the nature and characteristics of each Divine Person and how they relate to us. In this study, we will look at six topics: God the Father as Almighty Creator, The Person of Jesus, The Work of Jesus, The Holy Spirit, The Church, and the ultimate aim and goal of God's plan.

How to Use this Guide

Participants should read the chapters before coming to each meeting. Begin each group session with prayer for God's revelation and insight. Read the opening Scripture out loud before beginning the group discussion. The questions provided at the end of each chapter are merely to guide the discussion. Don't feel you must answer them all. There may be other insights from the group that warrant deeper discussion.🎗

Chapter 1
Almighty, Creator, Father

"I Believe in God the Father Almighty,
Creator of Heaven and Earth . . ."

Apostles' Creed

"Thus says the Lord, the King of Israel and his Redeemer, the Lord of hosts:

'I am the first and I am the last,
And there is no God besides Me.

'Who is like Me? Let him proclaim and declare it;
Yes, let him recount it to Me in order,
From the time that I established the ancient nation.
And let them declare to them the things that are coming
And the events that are going to take place.

'Do not tremble and do not be afraid;
Have I not long since announced it to you and declared it?
And you are My witnesses.
Is there any God besides Me,
Or is there any other Rock?
I know of none.'"

Isaiah 44:6-8

1

lobal Positioning Satellite (GPS) technology has revolution-
ized how we travel, observe weather, and even our everyday
lives. When I was growing up, my dad would get out the
U.S. Atlas, or a set of paper maps, weeks ahead of our vacation and
begin planning out the route we would take to our destination along
with the best places to stop to fill up the gas tank, eat a meal, or if it
was a particularly long drive, a motel room along the highway. Later,
when I was learning to drive, it was the repeated driving of different
streets and roads in my hometown that taught me how to get from
my house to school, the store, or my friends' houses. Every once in a
while, I might discover an alternative route because of road construction forcing a detour. Now, with the use of GPS in every car, we can
plot courses between any two points without reference to any major
locations, and even change our route on the fly, no matter how far
we are from familiar territory, to react and respond to dynamic traffic
conditions.

What makes this possible is the network of low-orbit, geosynchronous satellites constantly relaying information back and forth
from space to our handheld devices. The geosynchronous part is the
real key. These satellites orbit the earth at exactly the same speed as
the rotation of the earth, meaning that they remain over the exact
same spot on the earth's surface providing a consistent point of reference from which to relay positioning data. It is the unchanging
position of the satellite relative to the ever-changing position of the
traveler that makes the technology work. But there's something else
as well. Until May 2000, U.S. GPS satellites were designed with an
intentional "flaw" called Selective Availability. Selective Availability
meant that civil and commercial users of GPS technology were fed
intentionally erroneous, or inaccurate data in order to prevent the
technology from being weaponized by other nations or parties. Only
military units were provided the corrective data necessary to operate
with precision.

The lack of precision available widely was seen as a matter of na-
tional security. But, at the dawning of the new millennium, the ap-

plication of this technology to industry and consumers was deemed to outweigh the potential risks. Can any of us now imagine setting off on a journey, whether across the country or even to a new local restaurant, without first plotting our course on our GPS app? It's so common that it's become a standard feature of our cell phones, which in turn have all but eliminated the market for special separate devices.

As we set off on this journey of discovery through the foundations of our Christian faith, the right place to start is by orienting ourselves with the unchanging, immovable character of God our Creator. Like those geosynchronous satellites, our God is the objective point of reference for us as we move along life's path. But, our perception of God is often distorted, warped, or out of focus. We look at God through the subjective lenses of our own experience and assign to Him attributes we see in others. The Apostles' Creed begins, fittingly, with a declaration of who God the Father is, not based on our experience of others, particularly earthly fathers, but on who He has revealed Himself to be. We refer to the Father as the First Person of the Trinity, because He sends the Son, and from Him the Holy Spirit proceeds through the Son. Jesus describes how he was sent to do the Father's will, and that he does nothing apart from the Father. We worship the Triune God, and we begin our understanding of all things with Him. God is our objective point of reference from which we interpret our experience – of ourselves, of others, of the world. And the Creed begins with the beginning.

Creator of Heaven and Earth

It is important to remember that Creator refers to God in terms of function or work. While Creator doesn't refer exclusively to the First Person of the Trinity, it has historically been assumed as a primary role of God the Father. We shouldn't ignore the presence of the Spirit of God hovering or brooding over the primordial waters at the moment of Creation, nor the instrumental role of the Word of God through which Creation is spoken into existence.

In an economic sense, that is to say, functional, the Divine Persons have sometimes been referred to as Creator, Redeemer, Sustainer. While this is attractive to those who would prefer non-gendered references to the Divine Persons, an economic view of the Trinity has always led to problematic errors in understanding the Person or Being of God. The Ontological (dealing with the nature of being) View of the Trinity helps to maintain the focus on the nature of each Divine Person and the relationship between them. As we will see in the coming weeks, the Person and work of God are inseparable, yet there must be a distinction between the two. To reduce God to what He does diminishes Him even more than reducing a human being to a human doing.

On the other hand, the types of things that God does reveal something about His nature. The nature of God is to create—to be productive. This is one of the ways in which humanity has been formed in His image. We are made to be creative. When we can no longer bear the image of God, our creativity and ability to create is diminished. Like all aspects of human existence, we can't fully step into who we were created to be nor can we fulfill the role we were created to play apart from God.

Expansive Scope

That God is Creator and no one else and that, as Creator, He is also called *Almighty* and *Father* is especially significant. In some ancient and even neopagan religions, the creative forces are not held exclusively by a single deity. It is usually the case that other creation narratives outside of the Abrahamic tradition describe creation as either the result of conflict or a series of events that various beings contribute to. But to confess that we worship *the* Creator not only draws a hard and clear line, but it also establishes Him as from before all other things.

The Apostles' Creed states that God is the Creator of Heaven and Earth. This is a way of saying "everything." Between Heaven and Earth, you have covered the entirety of the created world. This is what would be called an *expansive scope*. Aside from the Creator Himself, nothing is outside the scope of what God has created. Anselm's ontological argument for the existence of God refers to God as the "Maximally Great Being," that is, the Being above which nothing greater exists. If there were a greater being, that being would be God.

Likewise, the Kalam Cosmological Argument for the existence of God is based on the following logical reasoning:

   a. Everything that comes into being must have a cause.
   b. The universe came into being.
   c. Therefore, the universe must have a cause.

God is that cause. But wait, who created God? Everything that has come into being, that had a beginning, must have a cause. But God is not something that came into being. God is eternal and therefore uncaused. Anything with a beginning, and therefore a cause, cannot be God. Ultimately, there must be something that caused all other things, and because the universe can't have created itself, that cause must be beyond the universe. That ultimate cause must be spaceless, timeless, immaterial, uncaused, and incredibly powerful. In other words, God.

Speaks to Revelation by Faith

God as the Creator of all things, and therefore being outside of this system, speaks to the necessity of revelation in order to know anything about God. If the Creator is separate from the creation and is outside of that closed system, there is a limit to what can be known about that Creator without the Creator Himself giving information. While the heavens may declare His glory, natural revelation (the knowledge that can be discovered through the natural world) is limited in what it can tell us about the Creator God. A machine may indicate a designer and a builder, but it doesn't tell us much about the personality, character, or nature of the one who created it. This means that self-revelation is required for any further knowledge.

Revelation differs from discovery in that it must be initiated from the object's side. No matter how high we build the tower or how powerful the telescope is, we will never see beyond the world we inhabit.

For us to know God requires the veil be pierced from the outside. This understanding is even supported by modern-day theories in physics, which hypothesize a curvature to spacetime that would eventually lead us back to our starting point if we were to attempt a journey to the end of the known universe. The curvature of spacetime imperceptibly turns us in on ourselves.

In a similar way, Saint Augustine of Hippo described our lives as "curved inward on oneself," *incurvated in se* (Latin). So long as we remain afflicted by the curse of sin, we cannot escape the inevitable inward pull of our own hearts.

This makes the self-revelation of God to Abraham all the more potent. Apart from God's free choice to make Himself known to humanity, we could have no hope of a relationship with Him. We would be grasping around in the darkness, seeking to put together the best idea possible to explain our existence and the world around us. In other words, we would be like every human religion throughout history. That God has made Himself known is in itself the greatest act of mercy and grace imaginable.

The question still remains whether we will receive it. The way we receive it is by believing or by faith. Those who talk about the restrictive nature of God's salvation by grace through faith in Jesus Christ complain that it's too exclusive. But they haven't stopped to consider this position within the framework of revelatory knowledge. God has shown the way to transcendent knowledge and has not made it secret. To criticize truth because we prefer to find our own lie is nonsensical and counterproductive.

Almighty

The Almighty aspect of God's nature applies both to His power and His authority. These have some profound implications when we consider the comparison of God to the deities of other world religions. It is a bold and important statement to say that our God is the Almighty One. There is an exclusivity created by this statement, which makes syncretism an impossibility.

Power and Strength

Let's face it, to be unimaginably powerful is a prerequisite for creating the whole universe. Even as powerful as the gods of ancient pagan religions were, the creative power of the God of the Hebrews and Christians is unmatched. The Creation narrative of Genesis 1 demonstrates that God exercised this power simply through speaking.

All ancient religions, particularly religions of the ancient Near East, had a pantheon of deities, each of which held dominion over a specified aspect of the creation. We are most familiar with the Greek and Roman gods and goddesses of war, wine, love, the ocean, the sun, etc.

The religions of the ancient Near East, within the context of the Hebrews and later Israelites, had their own set of deities, but worship revolved around four main entities. Baal was the storm god and male fertility god. His wife Ashtoreth/Ishtar/Astarte (who may have been identical to the Egyptian goddess Isis) was the female fertility goddess and identified with the earth. The relationship between Baal and Ashtoreth and their importance to ancient peoples' dependence upon a good harvest should become apparent. The third entity of significant importance was Dagon, who was considered to be Baal's father and was associated with grain and the wealth that comes from the harvest. The final central entity was Molech/Milsom/Chemosh, to whom the people would sacrifice their children and infants to ensure good fortune, prosperity, and peace.

In every case of pagan gods and goddesses, while they were seen to be more powerful than human beings, they were, nonetheless, limited in the scope of their power and sphere of control. Not so with YAHWEH. While the deities of other cultures required either the cooperation of or conflict with other gods and goddesses, the God of the Bible acts alone with sole discretion. He is not merely the god of the mountain, or the god of the river, or any other god of limited scope. He is the Lord God Almighty, Maker of Heaven and Earth.

Authority

Power can be usurped or used without authorization. Just because someone or something is powerful doesn't mean they have authority. Contrary to the claims of the post-modern worldview and propaganda, "might" does not "make right." This could only be true if there were no objective truth or moral right. If truth were subjective, there would be no standard for determining truth when two or more contradictory claims are made. The only choice would be to select whichever position can impose its will on the others. This is the "law of the jungle" rather than the law of the Kingdom of God.

One of the arguments for the existence of God states that God could not be God if He were not all-powerful, all-knowing, and all-good. A being that was not all-powerful could not meet the definition of *God*. Neither could a being that was *not* all-knowing. Although they might have all the power in the universe, they would be dangerous and nearly useless without the knowledge to apply that power properly. Worst of all is an all-knowing, all-powerful, yet not all-good being. This would not be a god worthy of giving worship or allegiance. This would merely be an evil, capricious, and possibly sadistic entity that, at best, might be placated or at least avoided.

Because God has created all things, and all things derive their being from God, it follows that His authority is all-inclusive. His power extends over everything, and His rights are exclusive and primary. Yet, the witness of Scripture also shows us that God freely allows His creation to exercise some measure of autonomy or free will. This is evident not only in allowing Adam and Eve the possibility of choosing poorly and eating the fruit of the tree of the knowledge of good and evil but also in the invitations God makes to people to follow Him, as well as tests where people must choose whether or not to obey Him. But in no case does the extension of free will to humanity supersede or reverse God's sovereign authority. Instead, human will is exercised under the umbrella of God's authority.

Father

How we understand the meaning of *father* should be shaped by God not by us. Because we are corrupted creatures, we do not accurately represent or reflect the image of God in any of the ways we are intended to. One of the ways in which we fail is through the role of father. Even if they sincerely try, earthly fathers will always fall short of a perfect example of the Heavenly Father. Just as Christian fathers should extend grace to their children, children in a Christian household should extend grace to their fathers and understand the flawed nature of their human caregivers by not holding them to the standard of perfection met only by God. This also means that we can expect more from God the Father than even the most excellent earthly father and, most especially, from a deeply sinful earthly father.

Tenderness/Nurturing

The biblical portrayal of God as Father goes beyond a mere authority figure. It paints a picture of a compassionate and nurturing God inti-

9

mately involved in His children's lives. This concept gives believers a sense of security and belonging, fostering a relationship characterized by love, guidance, and tender care.

Throughout the Scriptures, God is portrayed as a loving and caring Father who guides, protects, and provides for His children. This paternal imagery emphasizes not only God's authority but also His intimate relationship with humanity. The tenderness of God as Father is evident in many Old Testament passages as He guides the people of Israel. In the book of Isaiah, God is depicted as a nurturing parent, likened to a mother who comforts her child (Isaiah 66:13). This metaphorical language emphasizes God's caring and protective attributes, underscoring the idea that His love surpasses even the most tender of human affections.

Jesus encourages his followers to address God as "Our Father in heaven" (Matthew 6:9). This invocation establishes a familial connection, highlighting God's role as a compassionate and approachable figure. Moreover, Jesus uses parables to illustrate the Father's unwavering love and concern for His children. The famous parable of the Prodigal Son (Luke 15:11-32) exemplifies God's merciful and forgiving nature, portraying Him as a Father who eagerly welcomes back a wayward child with open arms.

Protection

The biblical depiction of God as Father is intricately connected with His role as a divine protector. Throughout Scripture, numerous references highlight God's commitment to shield and safeguard His children from harm. This paternal aspect of divine protection is a source of believers' reassurance and confidence. In the Book of Psalms, the imagery of God as a protector is pervasive. Psalm 91 vividly describes God's sheltering presence. Verses 1-2 declare, "He who dwells in the shelter of the Most High will abide in the shadow of the Almighty. I will say to the LORD, 'My refuge and my fortress, my God, in whom I trust.'"

The concept of God's protective care also extends into the New Testament. In his teachings, Jesus reassures believers about God's watchful gaze. In the Gospel of Matthew, Jesus encourages his followers not to worry, stating, "Are not two sparrows sold for a penny? And not one of them will fall to the ground apart from your Father. But even the hairs of your head are all numbered. Fear not, therefore; you are of more value than many sparrows" (Matthew 10:29-31). This passage underscores God's meticulous attention to His creation, assuring believers of His constant vigilance and protective presence.

The biblical idea of God as a protective Father communicates that God cares for His children and actively shields them from some of the various challenges and adversities they may encounter in their earthly journey. This divine protection becomes a pillar of strength, fostering a deep and abiding faith in the unwavering guardianship of a loving Heavenly Father.

Discipline

Proverbs 3:11-12 declares, "My son, do not despise the Lord's discipline or be weary of his reproof, for the Lord reproves him whom he loves, as a father the son in whom he delights." This scriptural passage emphasizes that divine discipline is a manifestation of God's love. In the New Testament, the book of Hebrews echoes this sentiment, stating, "For the Lord disciplines the one he loves, and chastises every son whom he receives" (Hebrews 12:6). The concept makes plain that God's corrective measures aim not at punishment but at the growth and well-being of His children, affirming the deep and caring love inherent in divine discipline.

The goal of discipline is flourishing not punishment. God's discipline, as outlined in the Scriptures, is not punitive but transformative with the ultimate goal of fostering human flourishment. In the divine economy, discipline serves as a means to guide, correct, and shape individuals for their betterment. Hebrews 12:10-11 reinforces this idea, stating, "For they disciplined us for a short time as it seemed best to them, but he disciplines us for our good, that we may share his holiness. For the moment, all discipline seems painful rather than pleasant, but later it yields the peaceful fruit of righteousness to those who have been trained by it."

Discipline leads to human flourishing because correction and guidance from a loving Father contributes to His children's moral and spiritual development. The process may involve challenges and discomfort, but its outcome is described as the "peaceful fruit of righteousness." This suggests that the discipline, when embraced and learned from, results in a life marked by moral integrity, spiritual maturity, and a flourishing relationship with God.

The truth is that human flourishing can only be fully experienced when we share in God's holiness. God's discipline is a transformative journey that aligns individuals with the divine purpose, allowing them to partake in the sacred and experience a flourishing life that reflects the image of our Heavenly Father. Whether we are actively trying to go our own way or accidentally straying from the path, discipline becomes a manifestation of God's love, guiding us toward a state of abundant and flourishing existence.

Discussion Questions

1. How do we diminish people when we reduce them to their functional roles? Have you ever experienced this? What remedies might be available to us when this happens?

_____

_____

_____

_____

2. What does God's choice of self-revelation tell us about God's nature?

_____

_____

_____

_____

3. What significance do you find in God's creation through speech?

_____

_____

_____

_____

4. What similarities do you see between the ancient pagan gods discussed, or others you've learned about previously, and our cultural priorities today? Has anything changed substantially? In what ways?

_____

_____

_____

_____

_____

5. How have your ideas about God been shaped, for better or for worse, by human parents or authority figures? How have those ideas affected your ability to have a relationship with God?

_____

_____

_____

_____

_____

6. Can you relate to the idea of discipline as leading to flourishing? Do you know anyone who has ever said, "I wish I were less disciplined"?

_____

_____

_____

_____

Chapter 2
Exclusive and Unique
(The Person of Jesus)

"And in Jesus Christ, His Only Son, our Lord, who was conceived by the Holy Spirit, Born of the Virgin Mary . . ."
Apostles' Creed

Now when Jesus came into the district of Caesarea Philippi, He was asking His disciples, "Who do people say that the Son of Man is?"

And they said, "Some say John the Baptist; and others, Elijah; but still others, Jeremiah, or one of the prophets."

He said to them, "But who do you say that I am?"

Simon Peter answered, "You are the Christ, the Son of the living God."

Matthew 16:13-16

Jesus said to him,
"I am the way, and the truth, and the life;
no one comes to the Father but through Me

John 14:6 (NKJV)

y wife was an elementary school teacher for fifteen years, specifically first grade. Occasionally, we would run into her young students when we were out in public places like the grocery store or a restaurant. It was always funny to see their reaction to that first glimpse of Mrs. Lawson out in public. They would initially freeze with a stunned look of confusion on their face. You could see the gears turning inside their heads as they tried to make sense of seeing their teacher somewhere other than school. We probably all remember that without even realizing it, we just assumed our teachers lived at our school. This was the only place we ever encountered them and to us that's who they were. As a pastor, I regularly experience the same phenomenon, but sometimes as much among adults as well as children.

When my son was three years old, he wasn't able to enunciate the 'p' sound in the word "preacher" and would tell people his daddy was a "creature." I always thought it was very fitting because I am, in fact, a creature made by God and limited in my knowledge and abilities. I liked this because even though it was his attempt to tell people what I did, he was actually speaking truth about who I am.

We so closely identify what we do with who we are that people often have trouble transitioning from one chapter of life to another. One of the most common questions we ask a person when we first meet them is "So, what do you do?" When we introduce ourselves, our job will almost invariably follow our name as the second thing everyone will know about us. In fact, we often wear our jobs as an extension of our identity. But to reduce a human being to something they do, a function they perform, does not do justice to the fullness of their identity. This is even truer when talking about God.

Certainly, what a person does—or at least how they do it—reflects who they are uniquely; however, there is an important distinction to be made between the person and the work they do. Each one of the Divine Persons is more than merely a functional role. Even though theologians do acknowledge there is an economy of the Trinity, we do well to first encounter God as personal, rather than functional. This is especially true of the Son, Jesus, who we most easily and readily relate too. This distinction becomes even more critical to the redemptive process when we consider that in his humanity Jesus is meant to show us what true humanity looks like.

Son of God

A son, especially a firstborn son, holds a unique and important place in the culture from which the Bible has come to us. Property passed from father to son in the patriarchal social structure of the ancient Near East, which included the Hebrew people. For the ancient Israelites, one of the most significant ways they experienced immortality was through their descendants by the male lineage. This was as true for women as for men. A woman needed to have at least one son, if for no other reason than that he represented her retirement plan.

Because all property—real estate, livestock, equipment—was held by the patriarch (oldest male) of a family, women could not legally own property. When a woman was born, she was a member of her father's household. When she married, she left her father's household to join the household of her husband, if he was the patriarch, or her father-in-law, or possibly her husband's brother. When her husband died, she became a member of her son's household. Because there were no companies or businesses other than familial households, there were no other employment opportunities or ways to provide for one's living besides participating in the industry of a household enterprise. If you weren't born into or married into a household, the only other possibility was to offer yourself as an indentured servant or slave.

A son would take over his father's household. This was a great responsibility and one that he would begin preparing for years in advance. The stakes were too high for him to learn the family business only after his father's death or even as his father's health declined. There were simply too many people relying on this future leader to leave things to chance. Eldest sons would begin transacting business with, and then on behalf of, their fathers for a number of years, beginning as soon as they were of age, usually around thirteen to fifteen years old. This meant that potentially, the eldest son could act on behalf of his father and the family business for decades as if he were the patriarch, even though he had not yet inherited that property or position. In this way, the son was both the heir and the agent.

Our modern-day understanding of a son is often limited to a child whom we love. While this meaning and understanding was undoubtedly true for ancient Near Eastern people (we shouldn't think they loved their children any less than we do), it was also not the totality of their relationship with them. But it did mean that the entirety of the father-son relationship was one of ultimate importance. Abraham, for example, lamented to God in Genesis 15 that his heir would be Eliezer of Damascus, a man born into his household but not of his lineage—most likely the son of a slave or servant. The significance of being able to pass to one's own offspring the responsibility and care of all that a person had, including all of those he was responsible for, cannot be overstated.

It is important to understand that daughters were also greatly loved and cared for. They were fiercely protected and honored. The title *Son* within the biblical context is so much more than just a male child. Although Jesus was born as a male human, his designation as the Son of God goes so much deeper than this fact. This is also why both men and women, boys and girls, can claim the office of an adopted son of God, and it is most correct to consider all believers as sons, rather than merely children or even sons and daughters. To give such attention to gender distinctions actually reduces the importance of women. First, within the ancient biblical context, a daughter would not have the same privileges or responsibilities as a son. Second, our sonship is by virtue of our union with Jesus Christ, who is *the* Son of God.

As the Son of God, Jesus serves as the ultimate revelation of God's nature and character. In him, the fullness of God's love, mercy, and grace is made manifest to humanity. The Gospel of John expresses this significance, stating, "And the Word became flesh and dwelt among us, and we have seen his glory, glory as of the only Son from the Father, full of grace and truth" (John 1:14). Jesus, as the unique Son, brings the divine into the human experience, offering a pathway to reconciliation and salvation.

19

One and Only

This distinction of Jesus *as* the Son of God is vital to make. In one sense, though a patriarch may have had multiple male children, there could be only one Son and only one heir/agent/successor. But in a true sense, Jesus is the only Eternal Son of God. While through Christ, we all are offered adoption as sons (regardless of our birth gender), only Jesus has always been the Son of God from all eternity. Because of this, Jesus is divine—he is God. Only God can be eternal, and Jesus makes it very clear from where he came. In the Gospel of John, Jesus repeatedly asserts his divine identity, affirming the exclusivity of his relationship with the Father. John 10:30 records Jesus saying, "I and the Father are one," emphasizing the unique unity and exclusivity of their divine connection.

It is by virtue of this unique and privileged connection that Jesus is able to offer us forgiveness of our sins, healing of our beings, and reconciliation with God the Father. In John 14:6, Jesus declares, "I am the way, and the truth, and the life. No one comes to the Father except through me." This statement emphasizes the indispensable role of Jesus in bridging the gap between humanity and God, underscoring the significance of faith in him for eternal life.

Jesus, as the one and only Son of God, encapsulates the core of Christian theology, representing the divine embodiment of love, redemption, and the pathway to eternal communion with God. In his letters, the Apostle Paul reinforces the exclusivity of Jesus as the Son of God when he writes, "For there is one God, and there is one mediator between God and men, the man Christ Jesus" (1 Timothy 2:5). Acts 4:12 reads, "And there is salvation in no one else, for there is no other name under heaven given among men by which we must be saved."

The relationship between the Son and the Father must be understood as primary with respect to our salvation. That is to say, while each of us must be in a personal relationship with Jesus Christ in order to receive and enjoy the benefits of his salvation and resurrection, this is a secondary relationship. The efficacy of our salvation by grace through faith in Jesus Christ is wholly dependent not on us but on Jesus as the Son of God. It is because of this relationship that he is able to offer us redemption, restoration, and reconciliation with the Father. It is a wonderful and necessary thing that you have a relationship with Jesus Christ; however, if your relationship were with a person who did not hold the exclusive position of Eternal Son of God, then it would be to no avail. This is why the exclusivity of Jesus as the Son of God is not only essential but also comforting.

Exclusivity is often the cause for criticism of Christianity from the world, which views inclusivity as a virtue. However, consider the episode from Lewis Carroll's *Alice in Wonderland* when Alice encounters the Cheshire Cat:

> Alice: "Would you tell me, please, which way I ought to go from here?"
> The Cheshire Cat: "That depends a good deal on where you want to get to."
> Alice: "I don't much care where."
> The Cheshire Cat: "Then it doesn't much matter which way you go."
> Alice: "So long as I get somewhere."
> The Cheshire Cat: "Oh, you're sure to do that, if only you walk long enough."

Apart from an exclusive relationship with the Father through the Son, determining which path to take is as arbitrary as picking any path to take. *Knowing* with confidence that a particular route is one that leads us safely to where we wish to go is a much better alternative than *wondering* which path will indeed get us there. By definition, following God is but one way. Either you follow God or you don't, and if you do not wish to follow God, then it doesn't matter much which way you go. But, if you *do* wish to follow God, then, wouldn't you like to know which path to take?

21

Our Lord

The declaration that Jesus Christ is Lord signifies his supreme authority, sovereignty, and divine rulership over all creation. Jesus' statement in Matthew 28:18, "All authority has been given to Me in heaven and on earth," makes an expansive claim. *Heaven and earth* is a phrase that indicates the whole of the created world. Heaven is the spiritual realm, and earth represents the physical realm. It is this authority that serves as the basis for Jesus' great commandment to his disciples, and through them to the church, to make disciples by going, baptizing, and teaching.

But this authority is also meant to be a source of comfort and reassurance. Immediately before, in verse 17, the Gospel of Matthew states that they worshiped him, but some doubted. The sense of the word used here is not that of a cynical skeptic but of someone not sure it's safe to trust what they are seeing. The implications for continuing to follow a failed would-be messiah were catastrophic, not only mortally but eternally. There would have certainly been fear of the ruling authorities, both religious and Roman, for their association with a name and idea that had already been dealt with in the harshest manner possible. Yet, here, Jesus stood before them. It seemed impossible, but if this resurrection were true, it would mean a complete vindication of everything Jesus had said, most especially the following words: "All authority has been given to Me in heaven and on earth."

As the Apostles lived in the power and presence of the Holy Spirit following the day of Pentecost, they no longer had any problem boldly proclaiming Jesus' sovereignty because it wasn't just something they knew; it was something they lived and experienced. The same can be said for the Apostle Paul, who encounters the Resurrected Christ on the road to Damascus. In Philippians 2:9-11, he wrote, "Therefore God has highly exalted him and bestowed on him the name that is above every name, so that at the name of Jesus every knee should bow, in heaven and on earth and under the earth, and every tongue confess that Jesus Christ is Lord, to the glory of God the Father." This Scripture underscores the universal acknowledgment of Jesus as Lord and emphasizes the worship due to him. Notice that this passage says nothing about willingly bowing or confessing to Jesus' Lordship. It merely says that this objective truth will be universally acknowledged by all of creation.

Can you imagine a fate more accurately characterized as hell than having no choice but to recognize the supreme lordship of the one whom you explicitly rejected? For those who reject God and Jesus Christ as Lord, this is their fate: that for all eternity, they must acknowledge the truth which they attempted to deny.

This would seemingly make clear that to confess Jesus as Lord goes beyond a mere acknowledgment; it implies a submission to his authority, a recognition of his divinity, and a commitment to live out his teachings and example. Faith and belief are not simply intellectual in nature. Faith requires action; that is to say, unless a belief is expressed through outward behavior shaped by the belief, then it is just an academic concept. This is what James means when he writes, "Faith also, if it has no works, is dead." (James 2:17).

Of course, we are familiar with the Apostle Paul's statement in Romans 10:9, "If you confess with your mouth that Jesus is Lord and believe in your heart that God raised him from the dead, you will be saved." But we may not be as familiar with the immediate context of verse 8 and that Paul is quoting Deuteronomy 30:14, which itself should be read in its own immediate context. Moses, in giving his final charge to the Israelites, reminds them of the Word of God and their duty to live according to it. He reminds them that they don't have to go searching far and wide for truth or guidance to live a successful life. God has already provided this for them if they will simply speak it and live it. The Word of God has been placed in their mouths and in their hearts—that is the core of their being, the essence of who they are.

Likewise, Paul is telling the Romans that Jesus Christ, the Word made flesh, has already shown them the truth and the way and the life; all they must do is allow him to shape the core of their being and live that out boldly through honest confession of the truth both in word and deed. This confession marks a transformative act of faith, acknowledging Jesus' lordship as integral to the Christian identity and salvation. It is the natural product and outgrowth of the internally transformed life.

Conceived by the Holy Spirit, Born of the Virgin Mary

The conception of Christ by the Holy Spirit and the Virgin Birth signifies the incarnation, where God takes on human flesh, bridging the gap between the divine and the earthly. It highlights Jesus' sinless nature, essential for his role as the sacrificial Lamb of God. The Virgin Birth is a foundational doctrine, shaping the Christian understanding of Jesus' divine mission and illustrating God's extraordinary intervention in human history for the redemption of humanity.

As described in Luke 1:30-38, the angel Gabriel announces to Mary that she will conceive by the Holy Spirit, emphasizing the miraculous nature of this conception. The Virgin Birth underscores the divine origin of Jesus, affirming his unique identity as both fully God and fully human. One of the crucial aspects of this conception is that it fulfills Old Testament prophecies (Isaiah 7:14) and establishes Jesus as the promised Messiah. Joseph, Mary's betrothed, was also informed by an angel in Matthew 1:20 that the child she was carrying was from the Holy Spirit. Beyond the simple miracle of this and the direct linkage of Jesus to God as his Father, why does this divine conception matter? What types of problems does this idea of conception by the Holy Spirit present? Could God have simply divinely anointed a human child and filled that flesh with His own presence?

Some might view the fact that Jesus was conceived without human sexual intercourse means that it was in some way pure or holy. But this takes a very negative, even dirty, view of sex between a husband and wife, which is not at all consistent with the biblical witness of God's designed plan for human flourishment. This view seems to reflect more of our contemporary difficulties with the topic of sex, which range from obsession to repulsion and shame.

Placing the focus here also opens the door for one of Islam's classic objections to Jesus as the Son of God rather than merely a prophet, which is that Muslims infer from a purely sexual basis of conception that Christianity must teach God somehow engaged in intercourse with the Virgin Mary in much the same way pagan mythological gods such as Zeus or Hermes were said to have done in stories and fables. Muslims rightly find such a suggestion blasphemous and, therefore, outright reject the doctrine of Jesus' Sonship.

However, if instead we think in terms of lineage and inheritance rather than acts and activities, we can understand how it was necessary for the God-man to claim parentage from both human and divine sources. Since only females of the human species are capable of carrying and bearing a child, that meant his human side would necessarily be his mother. Furthermore, since inheritance, which would include both assets and liabilities, was passed down from father to son, Jesus does not inherit any debt for sin because his patriarchal lineage does not come from humanity. Instead, Jesus' patriarch is God the Father, whose kingdom-estate is infinite in worth and has no debts held against it. In this way, Jesus could assume the fallen flesh with Adam and Eve in order that it might be redeemed while, at the same time, bearing no obligation himself for the debt of Adam's sin.

Various aspects of atonement rely on the divine and human nature of Christ uniquely facilitated by the conception by the Holy Spirit and birth from a virgin. In the ransom theory of atonement, only the One who owes no debt of sin, yet owns an infinite estate, can pay the incredible debt of sin for all of humanity, while, at the same time, only the One who represents humanity can make that payment.

Likewise, the penal substitutionary atonement theory requires a perfect, unblemished sacrifice *and* that it be offered by the one who requires atonement. When considering Christ as our mediator, it must be remembered that only God can stand before God and only man can represent man. Christ represents us before the Father and represents the Father to us. In this way, both sides of the covenant between God and humanity are fulfilled by the one God-man. It is as if God is shaking His own hand. The effects of this will be covered in more detail in the chapter on the Work of Jesus.

Discussion Questions

1. How does the multifaceted role of the "Son" within the biblical context impact your understanding of yourself as a follower of Christ and a son of God?

_____

_____

_____

_____

2. What issues, if any, does the exclusivity of Jesus as the way, the truth, and the life raise for you? Does this exclusivity bring comfort or concern? Has it always been that way for you? What implications does this exclusivity bring to your own life and personal relationships?

_____

_____

_____

_____

3. In what ways does the necessity of outward evidence of inward formation challenge some minimalist conceptions of confession and belief? Why do you think it is so popular to reduce Christian faith to intellectual exercises?

_____

_____

_____

_____

4. Why does it matter that Jesus was both conceived by the Holy Spirit and born of the Virgin Mary? Are these doctrines as essential as the Resurrection? Why or why not?

_____

_____

_____

_____

_____

Chapter 3
Effective and Final
(The Work of Jesus)

". . . Suffered under Pontius Pilate, was crucified, died and was buried; He descended to the dead. On the third day, he rose from the dead. He ascended into Heaven, and sits at the right hand of God the Father Almighty . . ."

Apostles' Creed

For I handed down to you as of first importance what I also received,

that Christ died for our sins according to the Scriptures,

and that He was buried,

and that He was raised on the third day according to the Scriptures,

and that He appeared to Cephas, then to the twelve.

After that, He appeared to more than five hundred brothers and sisters at one time,

most of whom remain until now, but some have fallen asleep;

then He appeared to James, then to all the apostles;

and last of all, as to one untimely born, He appeared to me also.

For I am the least of the apostles, and not fit to be called an apostle,

because I persecuted the church of God.

1 Corinthians 15:3-9

When we moved to Alabama in the spring of 2023, our house-hunting was varied and wide. We considered buying land and building. We looked at houses closer into town, and further out in the country. When we finally pulled into the new construction in a neighborhood near the lake, we knew we had found our home. In twenty-six years of marriage, we had never lived in a new home. Through six moves, there were always repairs and remodeling projects that came along with the first six to nine months in a new place. I can practically install toilets blindfolded; I've purchased and installed so many over the years. But this time would be different.

One of the things we loved about this new house was the landscaping and curb appeal, especially the large boulders placed perfectly near the corners of the house. This was a unique feature and really made it look as if the house had been there a very long time. It was an instant feeling of home. We later learned that this was kind of a signature design aspect of this particular builder. He told us he'd always just liked boulders and large rocks so he would collect them from building sites. After a while he accumulated quite a few and so he began to bring them and position them on homesites. The result was a little bit of his personality, and his story was left on the face of every house he built.

Any artist or craftsman leaves an imprint of themselves on their work. Painters have distinct styles and certain design elements, mediums, or subjects which can be used to identify specific artists. A writer has their own unique voice. Every job bears some reflection of the one who does it. While we are not the things we do, we do them in a way that reflects who we are.

Introduction

As briefly mentioned earlier, a distinction must be made between *person* and *work*. This is true of all creatures but also of the Creator. This distinction, however, is not a separation. In a sense, who God is is defined by what God does. Yet, God is more than simply His functional purpose.

In the same way that a human being is more than just what they do, even more so is the Son of God more than his functional role. Yet, it is impossible to understand who he is apart from the work he does. The shorthand version of this could be summarized like this: God is love. But we don't understand what *love* means until we see it demonstrated on the Cross. God is not merely love in the abstract; He is love in action. And not just any definition of *love* we wish to assign to Him. He is "cruciform love," that is, love expressed in the sacrifice and offering we see in Jesus. So, to understand *who* God is in Jesus, we must realize *what* God does in Jesus.

Suffered under Pontius Pilate

The inclusion of Pontius Pilate's name in the creed is important because it roots the Christian confession in an actual historical time and place. What has been lost to most of us is the fact that all ancient religions had foundational stories that were set in mythical and otherworldly times and places. This wasn't shocking to the people who followed these systems; it was just the norm. Today, if I began a story, "A long time ago, in a galaxy far, far away,. ." you immediately know I'm telling a fictional story that doesn't even pretend to have a basis in fact. But for the ancients, that wasn't the case. Some popular writers and commentators today like to point out similarities between the Egyptian gods, the ancient Sumerian gods, and the stories of both Jesus' birth and his resurrection. They say this demonstrates that Christianity merely borrowed ideas from older myths and religions to fabricate their own.

But as is always the case with such claims, what is important is not the similarities but the differences. And here is one of the most significant differences: Christianity is not a religion based in the "mists of time," in mythical lands, but in our actual historical timeline. Pontius Pilate was a real person, and there is documented evidence for who he was, when and where he lived, and what he did. The connection to a source outside of both Christian and Jewish circles would make anything about the Jesus story easy to contradict if it were untrue. The fact that archeological evidence for these confessions of Jesus as the resurrected messiah dates to within a single lifetime of the events they describe further strengthens their veracity.

It's one thing to lie about what happened hundreds of years ago on the other side of the world; it's quite another to try and peddle a lie in the city where it supposedly took place, while those who were alive at the time can still refute your story. Add to this the fact that those making the confession were persecuted and killed because of it; why would anyone tell an easily debunked lie that would lead to their suffering and possible death? And why would thousands of people flock to this group, abandoning their family connections? This is what the confession of Christ suffering under the very specific Roman governor helps to demonstrate—that this is not a fabrication at all.

Was Crucified, Dead, and Buried

At the center of the Christian faith stands the incarnation of Jesus Christ, and at the center of the Incarnation is the crucifixion. It is from this eternal reality that all of Christianity takes its shape. It is often so taken for granted that Jesus died, that it might be a good place to start by asking the question, "Why did Jesus have to die?" Or, perhaps, even asking whether or not Jesus had to die?

There was, in the last century, a popular notion among some intellectuals and scholars who saw Jesus merely as the idealized human that if only Jesus had not been viciously killed by the religious and political authorities, he could have accomplished so much more.

Such thoughts entirely miss the point of Jesus' work here on earth. Jesus' death by crucifixion was not an unfortunate accident, nor was it even the inevitable consequence of "speaking truth to power." It was, in actuality, Jesus' mission in stepping down from eternity into human flesh to "give his life as a ransom for many" (Matthew. 20:28). Yet, the fullness of Jesus' suffering, death, and burial is more complete than a single statement.

First, Jesus died, Hebrews 2:9 says, that by the suffering of his death, "He might taste death for everyone." Jesus being crucified in our place on behalf of the entire human race is called *substitutionary atonement*. Christ died as a substitute for us so that we would not have to pay the penalty for sin. God told Adam and Eve in the garden that if they ate the fruit of the tree of the knowledge of good and evil, they would die. This death was both an immediate spiritual death and an eventual physical death in the form of mortality, which had not been a part of human design to that point. Both of these were passed through the bloodline and lineage of Adam.

Sin is, at its most basic level, rebellion against God and His will. The natural consequence of living in a way counter to God's design is death and destruction, either immediate or eventual. This is not retribution any more than the consequences of trying to defy gravity by stepping off a high cliff or tall building would be. The consequences would come, but instead of making us pay the price, God, through Jesus, provided a substitute for us. Apart from the substitutionary atonement of Jesus, we are left fully responsible for our own sin and death (which is the consequence of sin).

Second, Jesus died too, uniting fully in our human experience and condition to create a new humanity. As descendants of the first Adam, all of humanity is tainted with original sin. It is a condition of fallenness and impacts every aspect of who we are. This is why no human effort can make progress towards atonement for the past, because whatever action is undertaken is spoiled by the stain of original sin.

This only compounds the problem and increases the obstacles between us and God. This is our "inheritance" according to the flesh.

There are those who wish to deny this doctrine, claiming that humans are born innocent, but this clearly contradicts the witness of Scripture.[1]

Through the Incarnation, Jesus establishes a new humanity and bloodline and is called the second Adam. This is the second work, so to speak, of both Christ and the Holy Spirit—to sanctify us. In the first, as we have demonstrated, Christ atones for what sin has been committed; that is, he redeems. In the second, he establishes a new humanity into which we are grafted; that is, he restores. We are adopted into the family of the Trinity. Hebrews 2:11 says, "So now Jesus and the ones he makes holy have the same Father. That is why Jesus is not ashamed to call them his brothers and sisters."

Further, Jesus died to destroy the power of death and the one who wielded it. How, exactly, does God die? How can the "Author of Life" himself experience death? Well, he can't, at least not in his divinity. But in his *humanity*, he did fully experience this very consequence of human sin. It was, however, something of a trap. Just as God's holiness swallows and destroys the impurity of sin, so too did God's power swallow up death and destroy its power. It could not hold him, and since he had entered into it and he alone returned from it. He alone now holds the keys that release whomever he chooses.

This aspect of Christ's atonement for our sin is called *Christus Victor*, which means "the Victorious Christ." Through his death, Christ made the once-and-for-all payment and sacrifice for the debt of our sins. Through his resurrection, Christ won the victory over the curse of death and offers that victory to us.

Descended to the Dead

Jesus' descent to the dead is, perhaps, one of the most misunderstood and confusing statements of the Apostles' Creed. This stems from a lack of theological teaching and a poor choice of words to trans-

---

1. Psalm 51:5; Jeremiah 17:9-10

late meaning into contemporary English. First, we should deal with how "descended to the dead" is most commonly phrased and how the cultural meaning we tend to assign to the words involved makes it an imperfect choice. "He descended into hell." For most people in twenty-first century America, hearing this statement conjures up images of fiery caves filled with bubbling lava pits and little red devils dancing around with pitchforks. Early Silly Symphony cartoons notwithstanding, our ideas of hell owe more to Dante's *Inferno* than the Bible. What most people imagine hell to be is a place of eternal punishment and torment for those who have either committed terrible evil or for those who have died apart from a saving relationship with Jesus Christ. The latter is not incorrect; it's just incomplete. From a scriptural perspective, there are three words we should know to understand this concept more accurately.

First is the Hebrew word *Sheol*, which refers simply to the place of death. Ancient Israelites understood *Sheol* to be a place of rest and repose, a realm of shadows dimly lit where the souls of those who had died existed in an almost dream-like state. This was the ancient understanding that developed over time with God's progressive revelation. During the intertestamental period, the idea of *Sheol* began to incorporate the belief in the resurrection as the ultimate hope and destination for all the faithful when they died. This was tied, at least partially, to God's revelation to Ezekiel in the Valley of the Dry Bones (Ezekiel 37:1-14).

Another developing idea was of a place to wait on the resurrection referred to either as *paradise* or *Abraham's Bosom/Side*. This was where departed souls awaited the coming resurrection in the comfort and bliss of God's presence. We see Jesus' reference to Abraham's Bosom in Luke 16 in the Parable of the Rich Man and Lazarus. In Luke 23, Jesus promised the repentant thief on the cross next to him at his crucifixion, "Today, you will be with me in Paradise." This place stood in contrast to where unfaithful Jews or Gentiles were assumed to go, which would have been a modified version of *Sheol* that was painful due, at least in part, to its separation from God's presence. But Jesus took this further in his teaching.

The second term we need to know is *Gehenna*. This term is mentioned by Jesus in Matthew 10:28 and Mark 9:43, warning against the consequences of sin. It is a place of "unquenchable fire" reserved as a punishment for those who have rejected God's Lordship. *Gehenna* refers to the Valley of Hinnom (*Ge Hinnom* in Hebrew), a place southwest of Jerusalem where, before the Exile to Babylon, Israelites would sacrifice their children as burnt offerings to the Ammonite god Moloch. These horrible acts of murder and blasphemous idolatry were part of why God brought the judgment of exile on His people.

God turned this into a valley of judgment on the Israelites and, as is so often the case in the Old Testament writings, the evil once enacted by the people ultimately comes back on them multiplied. First-century Jewish writings refer to *Ge Hinnom* as the torment that comes after judgment. When Jesus gives these warnings in Matthew and Mark, this title fits the first-century Jewish concept that also closely matches our contemporary understanding of hell.

One of the most erroneous popular understandings of hell is that it is the kingdom of Satan. This is not true. Hell, as Jesus seems to have taught it in Scripture, is a place where all rebels are punished, which would presumably include Satan and the angels who followed him. Far from being a current place (although it may already have been brought into existence), hell seems to be a place experienced after the judgment. Either way, our concepts of hell are not entirely accurate to that which the Apostles' Creed confesses.

The third term is *Hades*. Similar to the Hebrew concept of *Sheol*, the Greek idea of *Hades* was not necessarily a place of punishment or torment but simply the realm of the dead in the lower reaches of the earth (the created world). *Hades* is used in the early Greek manuscripts of the Apostles' Creed to convey Christ's descent into the lower reaches of creation, the realm of the dead, consistent with the understanding of *Sheol*.

Hades has been translated into modern English as "hell." However, Jesus' descent into *Hades* would be better understood as a descent into "the place of the dead" or simply "the dead." As seen in the parable from Luke 16 of the rich man and Lazarus, *Hades* is not a pleasant place. It seems to be a place of uncomfortable heat and dryness. Nevertheless, *Hades* was popularly used at the time of early Christianity as a general term for the place where dead souls resided. It was not to be looked forward to, but neither would it have been feared as much as we fear hell today.

The discussion of these various terms suggests that it is best to understand what the Apostles' Creed refers to as a descent into a holding cell type of space where souls who are neither in punishment for rebellion nor in a place of reward for faithfulness exist. In Ephesians 4:8-9, Paul writes,

> *Therefore, it says,*
>
> *"When He ascended on high,*
> *He led captive a host of captives,*
> *And He gave gifts to men."*

(Note this expression, "He ascended." What does it mean except that he also had descended into the lower parts of the earth? He who descended is himself also he who ascended far above all the heavens, so that he might fill all things.)

In verse 9, the phrase *he ascended* literally means "descended into the lower of the earth/land." From either a Jewish or Greek perspective, the meaning would have been consistent with those for *Sheol* or *Hades*. In 1 Peter 3:18-19, it is written,

> *For Christ also died for sins once for all, the just for the unjust, so that He might bring us to God, having been put to death in the flesh, but made alive in the spirit; in which also He went and made proclamation to the spirits now in prison.*

And in 4:6,

> *For the gospel has for this purpose been preached even to those who*

are dead, that though they are judged in the flesh as men, they may live in the spirit according to the will of God.

There may be some further examinations and curious questions we could explore from these verses, but the point here is that the author describes a journey undertaken to a lower realm by Jesus between the Crucifixion and the Resurrection to proclaim the initiation of his Kingdom, even in the most remote places. This proclamation's exact purpose and effect can only be the source of speculation: is there a basis for posthumous evangelism? Are these "souls in captivity" only from those who lived before the Incarnation of Christ and this procession of captives a unique occurrence that reset the cosmic playing field, or do they stand outside of time and space, representing the souls from all ages through the end of time who died apart from God? The Scripture is unclear on this point, so for us to assume any more than the Holy Scriptures reveal would be pressing the matter too far.

As is the case with many aspects of Christian doctrine, what we can know and understand is revealed to us clearly by Scripture; what we can know but not understand, we confess (how, exactly, does the hypostatic union of Christ's divine and human natures work?), and what we can't know through Scripture, we leave alone. We confess that according to Scripture, Christ did descend to the dead before rising on the third day and ascending into Heaven.

(See also other biblical references for Christ's descent: Matthew 12:40; Acts 2:31; Colossians 1:18)

On the Third Day Rose

The third day is significant in ancient Jewish spirituality and its understanding of death. In the first century CE, within the Jewish community, it was commonly believed that when a person died, an angel would be sent by God to help the soul acclimate and would usher them to Abraham's Bosom. It was thought the soul might be allowed to say farewells to loved ones and family before finally being taken from the earthly plane on the third day. For this reason, many would not consider a person truly dead until the third day after the seeming cessation of breathing and other bodily functions. This is also why Jesus delayed coming to Bethany to Lazarus, Mary, and Martha until Lazarus had been dead for four days. By performing the miracle of raising Lazarus from the dead after so long, there could be no question for those who witnessed it that it was, indeed, a miracle. Likewise, Jesus' Resurrection occurred in such a way as not to call into question whether he had resuscitated or, indeed, died and was raised again to life.

The third day also carries the significance of aligning with the time spent by Jonah inside the great fish. However, Jonah's experience serves more as a foreshadowing and prophetic sign pointing to Jesus' death, burial, and resurrection. The descent into the depths of the earth and/or the sea represents what is known as the hero's journey. This archetype echoes throughout literature and human experience, revealing a profound truth: only by confronting the darkest parts of reality can we overcome it.

This truth is written into reality's fabric, but it occurred in actual history in the person of Jesus Christ. Archetypes are rooted in a source, and here again, we find that Jesus is the source, the fountainhead, for all things, just as it says in John 1:3, "Through him all things were made; without him nothing was made that has been made."

But most importantly: Christ rose after having truly experienced death, after truly descending into the furthermost depths of all creation. The fact that death, Hades, and the grave were unable to hold him vindicates him against all false accusations and demonstrates two things decisively: he is God, he is the eternal source of all life and all things, and his Kingdom rules over every other power that sets itself up against him.

The figure of the Messiah was established in Jewish tradition as God's anointed servant who would triumph over every worldly power. Hundreds of others have led rebellions against earthly kingdoms that many believed to be sent from God. But every one of those would-be messiahs ended up dead.

For those who followed Jesus, those three days were terrifying and devastating. When Christ revealed himself as resurrected, the time spent with the disciples transformed them and gave a basis for the boldness that would come from the indwelling of the Holy Spirit. The most dangerous man in the world is the one you can't kill or if you do, doesn't stay dead. When Christ's followers realize that because he is raised, they too will be, nothing can intimidate them or cause them to diverge from the path on which he is leading them.

Ascended into Heaven

Perhaps the most overlooked aspect of our Christian confession in the Apostles' Creed is that Christ ascended into Heaven. With all of the celebration and fanfare over Christmas and Easter, very few Christians today are even aware of Ascension Day. Even with a resurgence of focus on Pentecost within charismatic renewal movements, few, if any, evangelical Christians celebrate what is the most essential act of Christ behind the Crucifixion and the Resurrection.

It would be more correct to say that all three, the Crucifixion, the Resurrection, and the Ascension, must be seen as equally vital. Remove any one and the others are diminished. As we've already seen, a crucified messiah is a defeated fraud. But without the sacrificial death, while the Resurrection is miraculous, no payment for sin has been made. But if the messiah then simply disappears like a vapor, we're left with an esoteric philosophy that doesn't connect to how and where we live in the present.

Because Jesus didn't just fade into the mist, we hold fast to something much more substantial and infinitely more connected to our daily lives. This connection can be thought of in the framework of his continuing threefold ministry as prophet, priest, and king. These roles are not just what he did but what he continues to do. The loss of emphasis on Christ's Ascension moves his work from alive and active to a past event, which is in complete contradiction to our confession of Jesus as the Eternal Son of God.

In his prophetic role, Jesus has proclaimed the good news that the Kingdom of God is at hand[2] and now delays his return, allowing people to respond to this message. Just like the prophets of the Old Testament, Jesus came declaring the coming of the Day of the Lord: a day when the poor will receive good news, the captive released, the blind receive their sight, and the oppressed set free. He also declared judgment on those who reject the coming Kingdom.

Now he waits. The freedom and healing he brings has begun already but will come in full upon his return on the Day of the Lord. But that day also brings ultimate judgment. Jesus' prophetic role includes his patience in giving time to all who will respond to the message.

A priest's role is to represent the people before their God and to represent God to the people. It is the role of a mediator or intercessor. This is probably the most neglected role of Christ today. Jesus being seated at the right hand of the Father gives him unique and exclusive access. We need no other priest because Christ himself intercedes on our behalf. This is beautifully captured in the words of Charles Wesley's hymn, "Arise My Soul Arise":

Five bleeding wounds he bears,
Received on Calvary;
They pour effectual prayers,
They strongly plead for me;
"Forgive him, O forgive," they cry,
"Forgive him, O forgive," they cry,
"Nor let that ransomed sinner die!"

When we pray in Jesus' name, what we mean is that we are offering our prayers through Jesus, our Mediator. We don't have to worry about praying perfect prayers (as if we could) because Christ perfects

---

2. Matthew 4:17

our prayers as we offer them through him. Then he joins our prayers with his before he presents them to the Father. John 17 provides some insight as to the way in which Christ prays on our behalf. In this, we come to understand that the relationship between Christ and the Father is of supreme importance to our salvation (redemption, restoration, reconciliation).

Finally, the King reigns in victory over all of Creation. Having defeated sin, death, hell, and the devil, Jesus has rightly claimed his throne over all things. As servants, heralds, coheirs, and coregents with Christ, we share in his victory over all the rebellious powers of this world.

Once again, the full impact of this reality may be a casualty of our lost emphasis on the power of the Ascension. Most Christians today will claim Jesus as their Lord and their King but may not honestly believe that his reign and rule over all things has yet occurred. Too many Evangelical Christians continue to look to some future date when Jesus will assume the throne of the universe when, in truth, he already has.

How can we effectively proclaim Christ's Kingdom if we ourselves aren't living in it? How can we convincingly declare that Christ has conquered all if we don't claim the victory he has already won? Yes, there is still suffering; yes, there is still evil in this world. But those are defeated foes; the Kingdom has already broken through, and that is what we are to represent and proclaim both through our words and our actions. The Kingdom is also coming. There is no unfinished battle yet to be fought; there is only the Day of the Lord in which he returns in the victory already won, and all rebellion is removed.

Regaining an appreciation for the Ascension of Christ leads us into a more dynamic and active relationship-based understanding of salvation. So long as we view Christ's work as a past event, then our very salvation can be thought of as a past event—an experience we had at some particular point in time—rather than an ongoing, present reality. Certainly, our conversion/new birth/regeneration is something we experience as the *beginning* of our new life in Christ. However, salvation is so much more than just our conversion. It is the ongoing sanctification of our being by the indwelling of the Holy Spirit. It is the victorious life of resurrection, and it is the intimate communion with God through our intercessor and mediator who has ascended on high.✦

Discussion Questions

1. How valuable is the historical role of Pilate in both your personal belief in Christ's life, death, and resurrection and your ability to defend it to others?

_____

_____

_____

_____

_____

2. Are there impacts of Christ's death you haven't considered before? What are they? Why do you think those haven't been a focus? Do you think they all carry equal importance?

_____

_____

_____

_____

3. Why would it matter enough that Jesus "descended to the Dead" that this would be included both in Scripture and in the church's confession of faith through the Apostles' Creed?

_____

_____

_____

_____

4. How does Christ's Resurrection validate his claims of equality with God and authority?

_____

_____

_____

_____

_____

5. What new perspective have you gained regarding Christ's ascension to the right hand of the Father? How does this alter your understanding of our present reality? Is this something you might consider placing more emphasis on going forward? How might you live that out?

_____

_____

_____

_____

_____

Chapter 4

Truth and Power

(The Holy Spirit)

"I believe in the Holy Spirit . . ."

Apostles' Creed

"But I tell you the truth, it is to your advantage that I go away; for if I do not go away, the Helper will not come to you; but if I go, I will send Him to you. And He, when He comes, will convict the world concerning sin and righteousness and judgment; concerning sin, because they do not believe in Me; and concerning righteousness, because I go to the Father and you no longer see Me; and concerning judgment, because the ruler of this world has been judged. I have many more things to say to you, but you cannot bear them now. But when He, the Spirit of truth, comes, He will guide you into all the truth; for He will not speak on His own initiative, but whatever He hears, He will speak; and He will disclose to you what is to come. He will glorify Me, for He will take of Mine and will disclose it to you. All things that the Father has are Mine; therefore I said that He takes of Mine and will disclose it to you."

John 16:7-15

"But you will receive power when the Holy Spirit has come upon you; and you shall be My witnesses both in Jerusalem, and in all Judea and Samaria, and even to the remotest part of the earth."

Acts 1:8

*D*uring my freshman year in college, there was a small lake on campus where some of us would go fishing. It was over behind the art building, and it presented a rustic, pastoral setting that felt as if it were miles away from a college campus. It was a great place to study, get away and relax with your thoughts, and (as we were doing) maybe even enjoy the excitement of angling. There was just one problem that occasionally arose. The lake was also home to a family of geese. I don't know how familiar you may be with geese, but they are not the most welcoming and friendly of creatures. Especially when there is a full nest.

Springtime is probably the most popular time for students to engage in outdoor pursuits, and it is also the time geese would be laying eggs and hatching goslings. That particular year, I remember the geese had nested along one of the longer sides of the lake between where we would access it and the far end where the dam was located. To get out to the deeper water meant walking around by the nesting location. It wasn't long before watching other student fishermen run from the attacking male goose was a more popular pastime than fishing itself. Geese can be surprisingly fast, are larger than you realize, and are remarkably tenacious.

When less aroused, geese appear to be quiet, lumbering birds. They waddle as they walk and do so in a way that seems not to have much purpose or intent. I suppose it's this deceptively docile facade that makes the reality of a goose attack so jarring. It's because of this seemingly aimless, meandering way of walking that some of the early Church Fathers referred to the Holy Spirit as "the Old Goose." Such a label sounds disrespectful to our ears, but the sensibility of it becomes apparent if you've ever tried to follow an old goose.

Jesus said of all born of the Spirit, "The wind blows where it wishes, and you hear the sound of it, but cannot tell where it comes from and where it goes. So is everyone who is born of the Spirit" (John 3:8 NKJV). Trying to follow an old goose, predicting where it will go, is like trying to anticipate the Holy Spirit. If we assume we know where the Spirit is headed and try to make our own way, we'll end up missing the mark, sometimes by an order of magnitude. All we can do is follow along as closely behind as possible without concern for whether we think we're heading in the right direction or not, simply trusting the process of the One whom we follow.

And, like the Old Goose, the Holy Spirit can surprise us with sudden bursts of energy and excitement. There's no way to predict, control, or manipulate what the Spirit is going to do or where He will go. All we can do is be attentive and ready to respond. A major part of this is becoming familiar with the One we follow. To truly know God, the Holy Spirit is essential to walking as a faithful and obedient Christian believer. It is an essential component for enjoying the fullness of all God means for us to experience both in this life and the next.

Introduction

The Holy Spirit is perhaps the most neglected and misunderstood Person of the Holy Trinity. As is evident from the lack of words dedicated to the Spirit in the Apostles' Creed, this was not a topic of great debate or theological reflection from the very early church. More specificity isn't given until the later Nicene Creed, but even there, the primary focus is on the person and work of the Son. The early church faced a much more significant challenge over comprehending the role of the Son relative to the Father while maintaining its commitment to monotheism, making the role of the Holy Spirit working in and through believers a less controversial topic. The seeming oversight or marginalization may also be partly due to Judaism's general acceptance of God's Spirit as an active and dynamic presence in, among, and through His people from the beginning.

In Genesis 1:2, we have in the account of Creation the reference to the Spirit of God hovering over the surface of the deep. Throughout the period of the Old Testament patriarchs, the Spirit of God was said to visit and inhabit Abraham, Isaac, Jacob, Moses, and Joshua to accomplish special tasks. This carried on through the time of the Israelite judges (leaders) and even early and godly kings of Israel. God's Spirit spoke through the prophets Samuel, Elijah, Elisha, Isaiah, Jeremiah, and others. It was the Spirit of God Ezekiel was commanded to breathe over the valley of dry bones in Ezekiel 37.

Ironically, the Person and work of the Holy Spirit has become a misunderstood topic as church history has progressed. There are those who have simply ignored this particular discipline of theology (pneumatology) altogether, often leading to a denial of one of the Persons of the Trinity and a weak and anemic church. The opposite extreme has seen excessive obsessions that cause dangerous and destructive errors to arise. But the witness of Scripture is clear on these points: 1) the Holy Spirit is coequal, coeternal, and One with the Father and the Son, 2) the Holy Spirit empowers the church and its members to know the Truth and do the will of the Father, 3) the Holy Spirit bears witness to the Son and does not draw attention to himself, and 4) the Holy Spirit draws believers into the life and unity of the Trinity.

Coequal, Coeternal

It must first be said that the Holy Spirit is indeed God. To some, this may seem so obvious as to be a strange statement to make. But even among those who confess God—Father, Son, and Spirit—it may not be evident in their thinking that the Spirit is a divine person coequal and coeternal with the Father and the Son. Many Christians think of the Holy Spirit more in terms of a force or power emanating from the Father or the Son. However, the Spirit is not an impersonal force. To think otherwise can lead to a form of idolatry in which we begin to see ourselves as essentially gods capable of wielding this power rather than understanding that we are the creation who are yielded to the Lordship of the One through whom all things were made.

It can be difficult for us to fully comprehend the personal nature of the Spirit because, as the Spirit, he isn't visible to us; but neither is the Father. Concerning the Father, however, we tend to relate to His voice or visible manifestations of His presence, such as pillars of fire or clouds, a burning bush, earthquakes, lightning, and other theophanies.[1] Even more than this is the particular character of the person of the Holy Spirit. The Spirit is the most subtle, quiet, and least likely member of the Trinity to draw attention to himself. Jesus tells his disciples in John 3:8:

> *"The wind blows where it wishes and you hear the sound of it, but do not know where it comes from and where it is going; so is everyone who is born of the Spirit."*

The early church Fathers often referred to the Holy Spirit as the "Old Goose." What seems like a disrespectful term actually refers to how you cannot predict which direction a goose will walk in. Fol-

---

1. A theophany is some visible and audible manifestation of God within the created world. It conveys the awesome power and overwhelming dread of coming face to face with the Infinite Almighty.

lowing a goose is a meandering path, yet the goose travels with intention. Just because we can't detect where the movement is headed doesn't mean it isn't directed. But as we'll see below, the nature of the Spirit is not to point to himself but to Christ, who in turn leads back to the Father.

Another indication of the Spirit's equal divinity is his eternality. This is present in the very first verses of the Bible:

> *In the beginning, God created the heavens and the earth. The earth was formless and void, and darkness was over the surface of the deep, and the Spirit of God was moving over the surface of the waters. (Genesis 1:1-2)*

Just like the Son, the Spirit is there even before the beginning. The Hebrew word translated as "moving" carries with it the connotation of a mother hen brooding over her nest of chicks. Once again, this description indicates a personal nature while simultaneously affirming the Spirit's presence and role in the act of creation.

Truth and Power

As we discussed regarding the Father and the Son, there are two matters to examine when we consider any one of the three persons of the Trinity: Person and Work. Since God is one in being, yet three in persons, it is tempting to define each member in terms of their work. There is a distinction between the persons without separation. Likewise, there is a distinction between the Person and the work without separation. For example, while the Father, Son, and Spirit are Creator, there are specific roles each Person plays in redemption, restoration, reconciliation, comforting, sustaining, so forth. There are particular functions the Spirit primarily fulfills as a part of the economy of the Trinity.

First, let's look at the role of teaching and instruction the Spirit plays in the life of the church and believers. John 16:13-15 states:

> *But when He, the Spirit of truth, comes, He will guide you into all the truth; for He will not speak on His own initiative, but whatever He hears, He will speak; and He will disclose to you what is to come. He will glorify Me, for He will take of Mine and will disclose it to you. All things that the Father has are Mine; therefore I said that He takes of Mine and will disclose it to you. (LSB)*

Jesus spent three years laying the groundwork through his teaching, example, and direction of the disciples. But he knew they wouldn't fully understand the how or why of what he was training them to do until the indwelling of the Holy Spirit fully enlightened them.

When we are filled by the Spirit, our minds are opened to the wisdom of God, and we are able to grasp the deep truth of His Word. This is a knowledge deeper than mere information. It is an understanding that isn't dependent upon education or past experiences; though neither discounts the value of education or experience. Again, the disciples were prepared with all that Jesus taught them. That knowledge was then activated by the living presence of God the Holy Spirit at Pentecost and beyond.

It should also be noted that what the Holy Spirit is leading believers into is the truth, which is ever unchanging through all eternity. The Spirit's witness will never contradict the witness of Scripture. Why? Because it is the same Holy Spirit who inspired the writing of Scripture. The truth that Jesus said the Spirit would lead into is the same truth he taught and the same truth of whom he said he was.

Additionally, Jesus is the Word of God. If anyone tries to claim they have a fresh or new word from the Lord that does not align with the witness of Scripture, we can safely conclude they are not giving a faithful witness, and they are a false prophet. The One who inspired the Word of God cannot contradict the Word of God but bears witness to Him. In this passage, we see how the persons of the Trinity are one in message and purpose.

Beyond enlightening the church and believers, the Holy Spirit empowers them to act upon that knowledge and understanding. Because the Holy Spirit is fully God, just as the Son is fully God and the Father is fully God, the full power of God is present in the life of the born-again believer. Jesus' promise in the Acts of the Apostles is that his followers will receive power when the Spirit comes upon them (1:8). Connect this with Jesus' teaching to Nicodemus in John 3:5, that everyone who enters the Kingdom of God must be born both of water and the Spirit.

In context, birth by water refers to biological birth. The birth of the Spirit draws a distinction that Nicodemus clearly did not understand, as we see in his response to the idea of a second birth in the preceding verse (v. 4).

The need to be born again by the Spirit is expounded upon by the Apostle Paul in Ephesians 2:1-5 when he writes, "And you were dead in your trespasses and sins. . . . But God, being rich in mercy . . . made us alive together with Christ."

Remembering that God told Adam and Eve in the Garden that if they ate of the fruit of the tree of the knowledge of good and evil, they would die, this was not a lie or an error. Mortality of the human body and soul was introduced at that moment. Illness and death were not part of God's original design. But in that very instant, the spirit of humanity died, and so every generation since is born physically alive but spiritually dead.

Dead men have no power. They can do nothing on their own. The life we receive by the Holy Spirit living in us not only gives us an ordinary level of power but goes beyond, bringing the full power of God. But we must also remember that because the Holy Spirit is God, a Divine Person, not an impersonal force, we do not wield this power. Rather, the power of God wields us. The only way the power is made available to the believer is through the absolute surrender of our will to the will of God. As we persist in this way, we can expect that the Holy Spirit conforms our will more and more to the mind of God. This is what we refer to as sanctification or imparted righteousness. It is the person of the Holy Spirit who primarily affects this change in the believer.

This is one of the great hallmarks of the historic Christian faith and the emphasis of the Wesleyan renewal movement that gave birth to the Methodist tradition. While our justification by grace through faith in the effective work of Jesus Christ to redeem us wipes out our guilt from sin, the Holy Spirit then not only brings us back to life spiritually (regeneration or new birth) but works in an ongoing way to transform our nature and to us the righteousness of God.

This is what the writer of Hebrews refers to when he says that Jesus, as our great High Priest, is able to "save to the uttermost." (7:25). This is the "perfect love [which] casts out fear" John describes in 1 John 4:18, and what Jesus means when he tells us to "be perfect as your heavenly Father is perfect." This is only possible by the indwelling presence of God the Holy Spirit because apart from his power, we continue to be unable to affect our own salvation.

Assurance

Another hallmark of historic Christianity and the Wesleyan tradition is the doctrine of assurance—that we may know that we are saved and that we may walk in that confidence. Although much emphasis has been focused on the doctrine of "eternal security" over the last two centuries, the fact remains that many, if not all, Christian believers may at times question the sincerity of their salvation experience. We don't always "feel" secure. For some, this can even lead to an extreme sense of guilt for not measuring up to the expectations of biblical teaching. However, this is where the promise of assurance can provide such comfort in every season of life.

Far from an attempt to forcefully deny what seems to be obviously true from our personal experience, this promise offers the privilege to go before God, seeking assurance and comfort in the reminder that we are not the ones who affect our salvation in the first place. In Romans 8:15-17, we read:

For you have not received a spirit of slavery leading to fear again,
but you have received a spirit of adoption as sons by which we cry

out, "Abba! Father!" The Spirit Himself testifies with our spirit that
we are children of God, and if children, heirs also, heirs of God and
fellow heirs with Christ, if indeed we suffer with Him so that we
may also be glorified with Him.

It is the birthright of all who are born of the Spirit to know that they
are a child of God. This is not a hollow promise nor an emphatic
declaration we repeat in order to convince ourselves. It is the power
of God alive in us, the Comforter to whom we are invited to reach
out and seek. This assurance is given both in the still, small voice and
the evidence of fruit he produces in and through us. Even though
there are those today who still teach or believe that we can't truly
know for sure, Scripture clearly teaches otherwise, and the Spirit of
God witnesses to us as we ask.

The Inner Life of God

The ultimate expression of this continuing work of the Holy Spirit
in the believer is that he draws us into the very life of God. When
we consider the Trinity as the eternal community, we discover a term
from the Greek used by the ancient church fathers to describe that
interaction: *perichoresis*. *Perichoresis* literally means "round dance."
The root *choresis* forms the base for the English word *choreography*.
The modifier *peri-* means "around," and it is used in English words
such as *perimeter* and *pericardium*. This term helps to conjure in our
imaginations the playful, loving, creative, and intimate interactions
of the Godhead from all eternity. It is out of this dynamic interaction
that the abundant nature of God overflows into creation to make
and sustain.

When we are incorporated into the body of Christ through salvation and into the church through baptism,[2] it is the Holy Spirit who
affects our incorporation into the *perichoresis* of God. We've already
discussed the filling of the Holy Spirit within us that takes place as

---

2.   "For all of you who were baptized into Christ have clothed yourselves with Christ"
(Galatians 3:27).

we are born again. In this, God Himself comes to dwell within our being, giving us His Spirit because ours has been destroyed by sin. But the other part of this is that we are drawn into Him. As branches engrafted into Christ, who is the true vine, we are made one with Him, and he is one with the Father, and together they are one with the Holy Spirit. The same Spirit who lives in me also lives in every other believer who has been born again of the Spirit. This means we are also one with one another. This will be discussed more fully in the next chapter on the church.

The inner life of God is not merely a static state. As the term *perichoresis* indicates and as the concept of relationship implies, the life of God is active and dynamic. We aren't issued an I.D. card when we are incorporated into Christ; neither is it merely our names being placed in some heavenly book. It's so much more than that. We are invited to actively participate in what God is doing. We are empowered by His Spirit to share in His life and work, to have our being transformed, and to have our identity renewed. In short, we once again become an image bearer of the One True and Holy God—He in us and us in Him.

Life in the Spirit

How does being an image bearer inform our everyday life? Let's begin by considering the three basic movements of the Christian life: worship, prayer, and mission. Worship must be understood as a responsive act; it is our response to what God has done in our lives. We were once dead in our trespasses and sin, unaware even of God's presence until, by His Spirit, we were convicted, convinced, and converted. By His grace expressed through the Person and work of Jesus Christ, we are redeemed through faith in this promise. By the Holy Spirit, we are restored and reconciled to God the Father through Christ the Son and now share in the inner life of God. The only logical response to this is to worship. But our worship is initiated by the

Spirit, who first convicts us and continually prompts us, even long after our conversion, to lift our praise.

Further, he fills our praise with power because apart from him, we have no power of our own. Finally, he purifies our praise, making it holy before the Lord. Christ is our Great High Priest and therefore stands at the head of the assembly as the true worship leader to carry us into the true Holy of Holies in Heaven. Our worship is offered to the Father through the Son in the power of the Holy Spirit.

The next basic movement of the Christian life is prayer. Scripture tells us in Romans 8:26-27

> *In the same way the Spirit also helps our weakness; for we do not know how to pray as we should, but the Spirit Himself intercedes for us with groanings too deep for words, and He who searches the hearts knows what the mind of the Spirit is, because He intercedes for the saints according to the will of God.*

The Spirit living in us shares the same mind that is in the Father and the Son. He brings through us prayers that are holy and proper to God. When we pray in the Spirit, it is not only our thoughts and our words that are offered, but our minds are also being conformed to the will of the Father. We are only able to offer these prayers to the Father because access is granted by the Son, by his perfect obedience in life, death, and resurrection. We offer our prayers "in Jesus' Name," which is to say, through his priesthood. As our sole intermediary to the Father, Jesus receives, perfects, and joins our prayers with his so that we can have confidence that they are received by the Father. We don't have to worry about praying the perfect prayer with perfect words, covering all the bases. In fact, as we've just seen from Romans 8, we can't pray the perfect prayer. But, by entering into the inner life of God, we pray to the Father, through the Son, in the power of the Holy Spirit.

The third basic movement of the Christian life is mission. The mission with which we have been charged is not ours so much as it is the mission of Christ himself; it is a co-mission. In Matthew 28, Jesus' final words to his disciples instruct them to continue the very mission in which he had been engaging for the previous three years. This command and co-mission are also based on Jesus' authority, as indicated in verse 18.

As we've already seen, the power to conduct this mission of being Jesus' witness comes from the indwelling of the Holy Spirit. The mission itself is to do the will of the Father, meaning that it is the Father we are truly serving when we serve others. Although people may be the beneficiaries of our acts of mercy, we must never believe it is humanity that we serve. When we do, we begin to allow human selfishness, pride, arrogance, and greed to establish our priorities and values. So long as we seek only to fulfill the will of the Father, then we are truly walking in the footsteps of Jesus. Doing all this, we see that our mission is lived out to the Father, through the Son, by the power of the Holy Spirit.

You should see by now the pattern that emerges from the life of the Christian believer. It is a life lived in the shape of the Triune God, a life lived to the Father, through the Son, in the power of the Holy Spirit. When we surrender to this pattern of living, it is not only our religious activities that take on this shape. When our minds are renewed by the indwelling Holy Spirit of God, we begin to see how the simplest everyday acts become acts of service, how service to God becomes an act of worship, and how worship is an offering of prayer.

Caring for our families through household chores, earning our living to provide food and shelter, speaking words of encouragement, and all the other simple human acts we engage in daily can be transformed in their nature to the extent we ourselves are being transformed. It is the presence and the person of the Holy Spirit who brings about that transformation as we cooperate through his grace.

The eternal purpose of God lived out in our everyday lives is a greater and more beautiful promise than simply an escape route from eternal torment. And it helps us to answer the question, what is our salvation for? Allowing the Spirit of God to enter us and thereby entering the life of God, we experience what we were truly created for, and God becomes incarnate in our everyday lives. Yes, we are all unique, and so is the way in which God chooses to manifest His presence through us. But with the Holy Spirit, we can learn and know the truth of what our unique calling is.🎗

Discussion Questions

1. What thoughts or teachings on the Holy Spirit have influenced your understanding of the third person of the Trinity in the past?

_____

_____

_____

_____

_____

2. Can you conceive of God entering into every act of your life, even the most mundane chores, and transforming their meaning and purpose? What would it mean for you to allow Him to do just that? How might that change your relationships? Your priorities?

_____

_____

_____

_____

_____

3. More than just agreement with a set of propositional truths, the new birth of salvation includes the indwelling of the Holy Spirit, who empowers, affirms, and corrects. How closely does this reflect your personal experience of salvation and the new birth?

_____

_____

_____

_____

_____

4. John Wesley, the founder of the Methodist renewal movement in 1700s England, said that "assurance is an inward
   impression of the soul, whereby the Spirit of God directly
   witnesses to my spirit that I am a child of God; that Jesus
   Christ has loved me, and given himself for me; and that
   all my sins are blotted out, and I, even I, am reconciled to
   God." Can you say you have this assurance? If not, would
   you like to know this? Pray to God to receive this from His
   Spirit, and continue to pray, believing He will answer.

_____

_____

_____

_____

_____

Chapter 5
The Body
(The Church)

For even as the body is one and yet has many members, and all the members of the body, though they are many, are one body, so also is Christ. For by one Spirit we were all baptized into one body, whether Jews or Greeks, whether slaves or free, and we were all made to drink of one Spirit. For the body is not one member, but many. . . . But now God has placed the members, each one of them, in the body, just as He desired. If they were all one member, where would the body be? But now there are many members, but one body. And the eye cannot say to the hand, "I have no need of you"; or again the head to the feet, "I have no need of you. . . ." But God has so composed the body, giving more abundant honor to that member which lacked, so that there may be no division in the body, but that the members may have the same care for one another. And if one member suffers, all the members suffer with it; if one member is honored, all the members rejoice with it. Now you are Christ's body, and individually members of it.

1 Corinthians 12:12-27 (LSB)

O ne of the hardest things my wife and I ever did was to leave our home church in Marietta, Georgia, to attend seminary in Kentucky. Although Mt. Bethel wasn't the church either of us had been raised in, or even the church we were married in, it was the church where we felt we truly grew up. We certainly had grown together and grown in our faith there. It was a place where we found friends, community, and a sense of belonging. As a young married couple in our twenties, it was helpful to see that others shared in our struggles and that we were not alone. These were the people we spent time with, vacationed with, raised our children with. But it was also the community God used to help me realize my ministry calling. They sent us off, launching us into ministry. The goodbyes were tearful and heartfelt; however, there was another embrace waiting on the other side of that exchange.

Our three years in Wilmore, Kentucky, was also a time marked by deep community. Asbury Seminary is designed for and committed to wholistic formation in community. We also arrived at a special time in the life of Wilmore First Methodist. We were among a group of families who arrived at the seminary in the Summer of 2011. All of us had been in another career for ten to fifteen years before answering the call to ministry and seminary education. I suppose the influx of young children brought a spark of life to the church, but truth be told, the permanent local members were also positioned identically to all of us at that time. That Fall a church wide social event was held at one family's farm, just outside of town.

My wife and I were both native Georgians, seven generations deep. Although we learned that Kentuckians consider themselves "southerners," they come from a very different culture. The Fall social was our first experience of the uniquely Kentucky burgoo. For those of you who are not familiar, it is a stew with a tomato base, containing beef, chicken, and pork as well as potatoes and assorted vegetables. But what makes it unique is that everyone brings something for the stew, and it's all put in and served from one large pot. Funny sounding name aside, we were fascinated as we arrived to see a thirty-gallon pot set above an open fire, and people bringing up cans of vegetable and portions of meat to add. To be honest, I don't really remember much about how the burgoo tasted, but what I'll never forget was the sense of connectedness we felt, the sense of shared purpose.

In both of these cases we experienced how important it is for human beings to belong. At its best, the Church is better than any other institution at providing this connection. This is because the Church is more than just a human invention. At its best, it connects us not only physically and emotionally, but spiritually, and not merely to one another. The body of Christ was, in the Incarnation, the way God identified with us and helped us identify with Him. The body of Christ, in the Church, continues this identification and connection. It also provides us with a place to live out an example of who God is and what it will look like when His Kingdom comes in fullness on earth. We often fall short of this ideal, but there is no place else where it is even a possibility. The Church is a privileged community because it is established by and built upon Christ himself. Though we seem to seldom live up to the highest and best potential, grace abounds, especially in this community of faith, to pick us up and help us press forward once again.

Introduction

The nature of the church has been the subject of much debate and discussion since at least the second century. The questions—where is the church, who is the church, what is the church—all have been examined in countless writings. It is, at the same time, simple yet challenging to define precisely what constitutes the church and where it is found. This is because it shares much with the One who is its head, Jesus Christ. Christ is both truly divine and truly human.

In the same way, the church is composed of both human believers and is indwelled by the Holy Spirit of God. There are both universal and particular dimensions to the church. It is both metaphysical and physical in nature. But keep in mind as we consider that Christ himself never ceased to be God, he also was defined by his particular human location.

Catholic vs. catholic

Let's get this one out of the way. The word *catholic* (lowercase *c*) means "universal;" when we confess our belief in the catholic church, we are saying that there is one universal church of Jesus Christ of which all those who confess faith in his grace are included. While we may talk about the church in specific geographic locations (for example, the African church, the Chinese church, the American church), what we really mean is the church in Africa, the church in China, and the church in America. There are no such things as separate churches. The church established and built by Jesus Christ alone is one body, regardless of location.

Likewise, there are not multiple churches based on ethnicity or race, nor based on gender, age, or any other qualifier. The church of Jesus Christ is not divided by denominations. And so, if you are united with Christ, you are also united with every other person who is united with Christ. We are all different. We all have different opinions, likes and dislikes, different languages, and so on. The true church transcends our differences and unites us based on one factor and one factor alone—Jesus Christ, who is the head of the church.

Certain denominations like to claim the exclusive right of being "the church." This is certainly the case with the Roman Catholic Church, as evidenced by the word *catholic*. However, this position has been softened, and recent popes, such as John Paul II, have extended a more gracious position, especially toward Protestants. The Orthodox tradition generally does not recognize the Roman Catholic Church or Protestants as practicing the orthodox (meaning "right thought") faith. Many Protestant denominations carry convictions that their particular doctrinal commitments define true Christian faith and do not consider Catholic, Orthodox, or even other Protestant groups part of the one true church.

Thankfully, focus on these divisions seems to have declined in recent decades. Instead, we are witnessing a realignment across denominational lines as those in each tradition deal with portions of their hierarchy that no longer hold to the primary tenets of the faith. The authority of Scripture as God's divinely inspired and inerrant Word and Jesus Christ as truly God and truly man who died a sacrificial death on the cross, was raised on the third day, ascended into Heaven, and is returning in glory to bring the fullness of his Kingdom has become the primary dividing line of any consequence. Today, some Methodists have more in common with some Presbyterians than either one has with other members of their own denominational bodies who don't confess the divinity of Christ or the authority of Scripture.

Holy

In addition to the church's catholic or universal nature, we confess that it is "holy." The Nicene Creed, which follows the same basic outline as the Apostles' Creed but with greater detail, confesses "one, holy, catholic, and apostolic Church." The word *holy* literally means "set apart for a special purpose." But it also reflects the integrity of the character of the thing described. God's holiness is an essential, inherent characteristic. God is holy because He is God; He is complete and lacks nothing. God's holiness describes His perfection and fullness in all aspects. The holiness of the church is derived from God. Because the church is founded and built by Christ himself, its nature is to be holy, but it receives that from Christ. As Ephesians 5:26 tells us, Christ has sanctified the church by his sacrifice, the washing of his baptism, and his word (paraphrased).

Christ's baptism, and our incorporation into that baptism by our personal baptism, is another biblical fact, though the understanding of this has been somewhat lost in recent decades of evangelical church history. When we look at the above-referenced Ephesians 5:26, it might be confusing to understand what Paul means when he writes that Christ has sanctified the church, "having cleansed her by the washing of water with the word." Equally, if not more, confusing is the earlier account in the Gospel of Matthew when Jesus overrules John the Baptizer's objection to baptizing Jesus by saying, "in this way, it is fitting for us to fulfill all righteousness."[1] How should we understand this?

The baptism John was offering was a "baptism of repentance." Jesus was without sin and, therefore, had nothing from which to repent. Jesus is demonstrating how the Law is fulfilled in him. He is identifying with Israel. But, more importantly, he is establishing a new meaning and new identity for those who come after him to be incorporated into. Like lepers who are healed or the blind able to see, after Jesus enters the waters of baptism, those waters are forever changed. Jesus becomes a new fountainhead, a new source for the living waters of baptism for all who would follow. His Baptism, given to the church in the Great Commission, is an incorporation into Christ.[2]

This isn't merely an individual incorporation, however. It incorporates the individual into the body of Christ, the community of

---

1.   Matthew 3:15
2.   Galatians 3:27

believers—that is, the church. As discussed in the previous chapter, we are incorporated into the very life of God by the work of the Holy Spirit. As Jesus told us in John 15, we are the branches grafted into the main vine. If we are connected to Christ, the main vine, we are connected to every other branch grafted into him.

It is impossible to claim unity with Christ while simultaneously being separated from any other believer. If we are not one with them, we have separated ourselves from Christ. The vine pushes life out into the branches; the branches do not possess that life solely in themselves. That life-giving flow is what produces fruit on each branch. If we attempt to separate ourselves from other members of the body, we then effectively block the flow of life from the vine, and it will be impossible for us to bear fruit. Jesus also warned in John 15 that branches that don't bear fruit will be cut off and thrown into the fire. Because it is Christ who makes us holy, we cannot separate ourselves from that flow. We must maintain our connection to the community.

The Communion of Saints

That community into which a believer is incorporated is what we refer to when we talk about the communion of saints. *Communion* is a word often used today solely within the context of religious observation, most commonly in reference to the sacrament of Holy Communion, the Lord's Supper, or the Eucharist.[3] It is also less frequently used to describe a grouping of churches, such as the Worldwide Anglican Communion. But at its heart, the word *communion* means to share the very essence of our lives and beings in the closest way possible.

In a highly individualist culture such as ours in North America, the idea of intimacy of thoughts, feelings, experiences, and sympa-

---

3. *Eucharist* is a Greek word from *eucharisto*, which means "thanksgiving" or "to give thanks." It is an interesting concept to ponder that the biblical text uses this term while so many churches today treat the observance of this holy mystery as a solemn and sad occasion, focusing more on the solemnity of Christ's death than his victorious resurrection.

thies is often met with resistance, even within nuclear families. It is not uncommon for us to have experienced or know someone who has experienced an emotionally distant parent. But even for those who have a culture of deep sharing within their immediate family members, vulnerability with those outside of the immediate household is an unsettling proposition. But this is exactly what the church is supposed to be; we regrettably choose not to participate in it.

It is understandable, however, why many would be hesitant to do so. Our misunderstanding of the church reaches far and has shaped how the institution and communities have been formed. For communion to take place, there must be trust, and trust must be built. But, if we, the believers who comprise the body of Christ, are the church, who then will build that trust? If we look to some outside institutional body, some third-party organization offering to be "*The* Church," to step in and fix the situation, we will never see it done. It is up to each of us to reach out to one another as bands of brothers and sisters to begin the work of building both trust and accountability. Then, we reach out to encourage others to band together and further encourage these groups to reach out to one another.

Together, we look to those anointed and appointed to lead the body, to extend our trust and, ultimately, hold them accountable. Accountability implies and requires a standard for intent and behavior. Where does that standard come from? From the only source of truth: from God through His Word. But if we are to administer this standard, we must know it and know it well. The invitation to communion comes with this responsibility. Otherwise, we will attempt to exercise authority and accountability with ignorance, which can be incredibly destructive, or surrender in ignorance to others' unchecked and unknown authority, which can be incredibly dangerous.

But our communion isn't just with those in our immediate circle. As we have seen, the church is a universal body that spans the entire globe. We are connected in Christ not only to those whom we see each Sunday, with whom we share a denominational affiliation, or even the entire church in our state or nation, but in Christ with all believers from every nation, tribe, language, and culture. Even more, the communion of saints reaches beyond the limitations of time.

Traditionally, the terms *church militant* and *church triumphant* have referred to those believers still here on Earth who are alive physically and those who have completed their mortal race and are now in Heaven with the Father and the Son. As the church militant, we continue to stand firm in the daily battle, obediently following where our Lord leads. But we are also surrounded by a great cloud of witnesses who stand before the throne of grace and share in our triumphs and sorrows. Because all believers are made alive in Christ, those whose mortal bodies have died still live in him. We too live in Christ and share in the intimate communion they have with the Father, Son, and Holy Spirit.

To bring this concept full circle, there are few times when our present experience of the communion of saints is more profound than when we celebrate and partake in the sacrament of holy communion. A sacrament is the mediation of the divine presence to us through a created means to which we can relate. Just as the woman with the issue of blood touched the hem of Jesus' garment in faith and was healed, the bread and cup of holy communion provide us a point of contact where our faith becomes active.

It is Christ who gives us himself so that we may offer his sacrifice back to the Father. Through this exchange, we come into the presence of Christ. When Christ is present among us, so too are all who are present with Christ. The table of the Lord in the sacrament is a foreshadowing and foretaste of the wedding feast of the lamb that will come at the end of time. Until then, this meal is the closest we can come to communion with all those who have joined the church triumphant.

Forgiveness of Sins

The work of Jesus Christ, his life, death, and resurrection, provide the necessary power for the salvation of sinners. The forgiveness of sins is only possible because of the work of Jesus Christ, as outlined in chapter 3. His divine nature, his human nature, and his sinless life of perfect obedience to the will of the Father all combine to make him the only one who can provide the necessary and adequate sacrifice for the penalty of sin. His resurrection provides the ultimate victory that has broken the power of sin over any and all who are in Christ. The sending of the Holy Spirit to the church transforms and remakes the being of believers as we cooperate with that grace to purge us of the being of sin, and our habits and desires are conformed to the heart of God.

With the ultimate hope of resurrection and glorification (to be discussed in greater detail in the following chapter), this comprises the totality of what we call *salvation*. Salvation is often understood only in terms of the forgiveness of our sins or justification. Sometimes, it may also be understood to include the new birth, of being born again, or regeneration.

We've already touched on the more complete understanding of *salvation* indirectly through our discussion of life in the Holy Spirit and what it means to be part of the communion of saints. But while we may need to recover this comprehensive view of salvation, it cannot be overlooked that none of the later stages can begin until we are washed clean and receive forgiveness for what has been.

It may seem that forgiveness of sins should be included in the work of Jesus, and there is a valid case for that. However, forgiveness isn't merely a one-time event. Forgiveness is a state of being. Once we receive the grace of God in Jesus Christ through faith in Jesus Christ, we enter a state of grace and forgiveness. The church is the context in which we live in that state of being. What's more, through the ministry of the church, as the body of Christ indwelled by his Spirit, we receive the forgiveness offered by that grace through faith. In John 20:21-23, the resurrected Christ comes to his disciples:

> So Jesus said to them again, "Peace be with you; as the Father has sent Me, I also send you." And when He had said this, He breathed on them and said to them, "Receive the Holy Spirit. If you forgive

the sins of any, their sins have been forgiven them; if you retain the sins of any, they have been retained."

Jesus also taught in Matthew 18:18: "Truly I say to you, whatever you bind on earth shall have been bound in heaven; and whatever you loose on earth shall have been loosed in heaven."

What are we to make of these statements? First, it should be noted that this authority that Jesus is delegating is not given just to an exclusive group of leaders. Yes, the disciples, who were later apostles,[4] were privileged in the initial authority they received by their direct witness to Christ's life, death, and resurrection. But they were merely representatives of the church that Jesus would be building through Pentecost and the continued proclamation of the gospel truth throughout the world.

Second, we must again remember that the church is not an institution or organization but the community of believers, the body of those who are in Christ. The church is not a third party—you, me, and the church. No, we, together with every other believer, are the church.

Finally, the church is the continuing incarnation of Christ in the world. The one defining characteristic of the Christian faith is the Incarnation of the Eternal, Infinite, Almighty God. Incarnation comes from the Latin *carne*, meaning "flesh." It is the basis for the name of the carnation flower, so named because of the primarily pink color of its petals. It is also found in the Spanish word for meat, as in the Mexican dish *carne asada*. To be incarnate means to embody, to put into a tangible form that other physical beings can access.

We've already discussed the importance of Christ's coming in the flesh and our need for a point of contact. From that standpoint we can understand the importance of an enduring representative of Christ in the world to carry on the message and mission of the Kingdom. Paul writes in 2 Corinthians 5:18-20:

---

4. The Greek word *apostolos* means "one who is sent out." A disciple is a student. Once the disciples were sent out by Jesus by the Great Commission, they became apostles. So too are all who live by faith in Christ, both disciples who learn and apostles sent into mission.

Now all these things are from God, who reconciled us to Himself through Christ and gave us the ministry of reconciliation, namely, that God was in Christ reconciling the world to Himself, not counting their trespasses against them, and He has committed to us the word of reconciliation. Therefore, we are ambassadors for Christ, as though God were making an appeal through us; we beg you on behalf of Christ, be reconciled to God.

It should be clear that the ministry of the church is a continuation of the ministry of Christ. He entrusts to his followers his ministry. Because it is his, it is conducted according to his standards, by his authority and power, and on his behalf. The church then is the ambassador of Christ empowered by the Spirit. As embodied believers, we are the continuation of his incarnational presence, but only to the extent that we are surrendered to and filled by the Holy Spirit.

With that established, we can now also see how and why the church is the point of contact for people to come to and receive the forgiveness of their sins through Jesus Christ. This should not be surprising because the only other alternative is for people to have random existential experiences of a nebulous transcendental nature with a "spirit in the sky" type deity. Once again, the church does not mean an institutional or denominational body, nor an elevated "professional" Christian, but the communion of saints is represented by its Spirit-filled members. This reality, though, should set in our minds the great responsibility we bear in fulfilling the Great Commission and the ministry of reconciliation, which includes the forgiveness of sins.

If you are given pause at the idea of accepting this authority and responsibility, that is as it should be. Being a member of Christ's body, his holy catholic church, is in fact no trifling matter. Anyone not made slightly uncomfortable by the prospect of all it entails has most likely not fully contemplated precisely what it is they have been called to. However, it should also not be lost that none of this is accomplished apart from Christ himself. So, we also can receive comforting assurance that he alone is the sovereign one, he alone is the power, and he alone gets the glory.

73

Discussion Questions

1. What are some of the ways the catholic nature of the church has been hindered in the recent past? Does the very fact that the word *catholic*, meaning "universal," has become used to exclusively refer to one specific group seem ironic to you?

    _____

    _____

    _____

    _____

2. What are the implications of the church being both one *and* universal? How should this inform our approach to Christians around the world? How might this impact the other identities we adopt (cultural, political, economic, etc.)?

    _____

    _____

    _____

    _____

3. In this chapter we have discussed the sacraments of baptism and holy communion within the context of the church. This is fitting as these gifts are given to the church by Christ in Scripture as marks of the church and privileged ways of experiencing his presence. The church, too, is established by Christ in Scripture to be his continuing presence in the world. How might this view of these sacraments shape your understanding of the church and empower you being part

of the body of Christ? How does this dynamic and spiritually engaged model of the church differ from some other models of an institution or assembly of individuals?

_____

_____

_____

_____

_____

4. Does the church as the point of contact provided by Christ for the forgiveness of sins give you a more sober consideration of our responsibility as believers and members of Christ's body? How so?

_____

_____

_____

_____

_____

Chapter 6
The End

(Heaven and Earth)

"From there he shall come to judge the living and the dead. I believe in . . . the resurrection of the body and the life everlasting. Amen."

Apostles' Creed

For I consider that the sufferings of this present time are not worthy to be compared with the glory that is to be revealed to us. For the anxious longing of the creation waits eagerly for the revealing of the sons of God. For the creation was subjected to futility, not willingly, but because of Him who subjected it, in hope that the creation itself also will be set free from its slavery to corruption into the freedom of the glory of the children of God. For we know that the whole creation groans and suffers the pains of childbirth together until now. And not only this, but also we ourselves, having the first fruits of the Spirit, even we ourselves groan within ourselves, waiting eagerly for our adoption as sons, the redemption of our body.

Romans 8:18-23

hen we were first married, Lindy and I loved to visit Walt Disney World in Orlando, Florida. Yes, I know there are lots of jokes about adults without kids who are obsessed with Disney, but we were practically kids ourselves at the time. Lindy had grown up spending two weeks every year at the Fort Wilderness Campground. During that era, we found the Walt Disney World Resort property to offer the highest level of quality service and to be a dependable vacation destination. Beyond that, living just north of Atlanta, it was an easy and short enough drive for two twenty-somethings to frequently make an escape from the new realities of adult responsibilities. For all these reasons, it made sense for us to purchase annual passes to the parks. They paid for themselves after seven days.

One year however, we decided to try something different and visit the eastern shore of the Chesapeake Bay in Virginia. In the early days of the internet, travel information was sparse, but we managed to locate a KOA campground right on the water. Borrowing Lindy's grandparents' camper, we set our plan for adventure in motion. Again, these were pre-GPS days and printed maps, or at least printed MapQuest pages, were the standard. We plotted the course, planned our first night's stay along I-95 north, and counted down the days. As we were headed out the door early Saturday morning, Lindy went to the kitchen drawer, pulled out our Disney Annual Passes, and as she placed them in her purse said, "Just in case."

Our route north, which should be noted is the opposite direction from Orlando, took us through Raleigh, North Carolina. It was here that the journey took its first wrong turn, literally. We were confused by Raleigh's Belt Line perimeter and had to exit in order to turn around. Narrow residential streets and a small bank parking lot led to a high stress maneuver which resulted in broken pipes under the camper, thus putting the bathroom out of commission. The delay involved also caused us to be off our pace. When we finally did get back underway with the sun quickly setting, we knew there was no way we were going to make our planned overnight. Luckily,

Lindy was able locate another interstate side campground. We pulled in with heavy eyelids, but certain that the day ahead would offer the chance to get back on track and make repairs when we arrived at our destination.

We awoke the next morning in the middle of a tobacco field. But at least there was a bathhouse where we could shower and pre-pare to be on our way. The remainder of the journey northward on I-95 was uneventful. We exited with only an hour and a half to our destination. Rural Virginia in the late 1990's was still the kind of place where everything was closed on Sundays, and the people didn't work outside. This gave the whole drive along the local road a creepy feeling of foreboding. As we pulled up to the bayside campground it became clear the pictures posted on their website were about twenty years out of date. Within four hours we were back on the road, hav-ing fortunately found the one open convenient store where we were able to use a payphone to secure a campsite at Fort Wilderness. It would still be one more overnight stay along I-95 before we limped onto Disney property, but when we arrived a great sense of relief came over us both. I was able to make the necessary repairs to the camper, and we enjoyed a stress-free week.

It's important to know where we are going in life, and even more important to be prepared. Our goal or aim determines how we define success and what we do to achieve that success. If we're aiming at the wrong target, we can succeed in hitting it but still fail. We need the best maps possible to point us in the right direction; but we also need to understand the destinations. Had Lindy and I better understood where we were going, we might have avoided a lot of hassle, or pos-sibly found other accommodations that would have caused Virginia to work out for us. But because we were prepared, we were able to pivot and make the call that salvaged our week.

Introduction

"There are certain words one simply must know." This statement from Dr. David Bauer, the Chair of Biblical Studies at Asbury Theological Seminary and my instructor of Inductive Bible Study, has stuck with me because of the understated and humble way it was spoken. The context described Dr. Bauer's experience heading up the translation committee for the Gospel of Matthew for a recent English translation intended to be at a fourth grade reading level. The word in question had been *repentance*, which continually triggered the program to flag words that exceeded this parameter. Although *repentance* is considered a word above a fourth grade reading level, Dr. Bauer (accurately, I believe) asserts the fact that there simply are certain ideas, and the words that convey them, we must know to accept the Christian faith sincerely.

While I wouldn't put the Greek word *telos* in exactly that same category, I would say it is a word that, if we can learn it, conveys a powerful idea that will drive a great deal of joy into our lives. *Telos* is a special word because of the multidimensional aspects of its meaning. It conveys, alternatively and at once:

1. a point of time marking the end of a duration, end, termination, cessation;

2. the last part of a process, close, conclusion;

3. finally, to the end, to the last;

4. the goal toward which a movement is being directed, end, goal, outcome;

5. last in a series, rest, remainder.

As such, *telos* conveys not only the idea of the end of a process, journey, or effort but also the purpose for it, the goal or aim toward which all things in the process, journey, or effort were directed, as well as how it is finally accomplished. *Telos* answers all of the critical questions: What? When? Where? Why? and How?

Similarly, we see in Jesus' teaching in John 14:6 that he is the way, the truth, and the life. As the way, he is where we are directed to go. As the truth, he is what we are directed towards as well as why we are traveling this way in the first place. As the life, he is the how that empowers our ability to travel the way to the truth.

He is the source of all things:

> *All things came into being through Him and apart from Him nothing came into being that has come into being (John 1:3).*

> *For by Him all things were created, both in the heavens and on earth, visible and invisible, whether thrones or dominions or rulers or authorities—all things have been created through Him and for Him (Colossians 1:16).*

He is the sustainer of all things:

> *For in Him we live and move and exist (Acts 17:28).*

He is the end of all things:

> *I press on toward the goal for the prize of the upward call of God in Christ Jesus (Philippians 3:14).*

> *For I determined to know nothing among you except Jesus Christ and Him crucified (1 Corinthians 2:2).*

From the triune Godhead flows the love that, by its nature, sacrifices itself to create, redeem, restore, and reconcile. It is the same God to whom we are being reconciled. Our journey is back toward the God from whom we received our very existence and against whom we rebelled. So, our source becomes our goal and our "chief end."[1] But He is also the only way by which we are able to arrive safely at our destination. In the final assessment, our *telos* is God Himself and

---

1. The first question of the Westminster Shorter Catechism is "What is the chief end of man?" with the response, "Man's chief end is to glorify God, and to enjoy him forever."

particularly Jesus Christ through whom, by whom, and for whom we were created and redeemed.

Coming to Judge the Living and the Dead

As previously discussed, Jesus is currently seated at the right hand of God the Father in Heaven. This means that Jesus' Kingdom has been initiated and is a current reality.[2] This is essential context for what is to come. When Jesus first came in the flesh and initiated an earthly ministry, the Bible says he "began to preach and say, 'Repent for the Kingdom of Heaven is at hand." (Matthew 4:17). (Incidentally, this is the identical, word-for-word message of John the Baptizer in Matthew 3:2.) Not only does this show the continuity of the message from the Old Covenant prophets–John being the last in that line–with the New Covenant, that is Jesus, but it also demonstrates that Jesus in his coming brought with him the Kingdom of Heaven.

Think of it this way: if the almighty, all glorious king has come to where you are, he automatically brings his kingdom with him. The initiation of this kingdom was through his passion and death. His ascension to the throne of heaven only came after his descent to the dead and his return to the earth from the dead. Just like we discussed in Week Three, Jesus' dominion is absolute and without limitation.

In much the same way that we have a wrong cultural understanding of hell, we also misunderstand the concept of heaven. We think of Earth as "down here" and heaven as "up there," as if it were in the sky or outer space. Ironically, this imagery is more closely related to an ancient Near Eastern view of the cosmos than a modern scientific one. In the ancient Near East, the part of the world centered around the land of Israel, most cultures viewed Earth as a disk that rested on

---

2.   Ephesians 2:6: "And raised us up with Him, and seated us with Him in the heavenly places in Christ Jesus."

Philippians 2:9: "For this reason also, God highly exalted Him, and bestowed on Him the name which is above every name." Hebrews 1:3, 10:12, 12:2.

the "pillars of the earth," located in the underworld, with the dome of the sky stretched out over the earth. Heaven was thought to be beyond the dome of the sky. This is an entirely human-centered way of seeing the world and its place in the heavens. It begins where we stand and observe from that point.

As we have gained the ability to observe our world from other vantage points, the truth that this imagery describes is no less valid. God's dwelling is still "higher" than ours, just as His ways are higher than our ways. But by letting go of the literal sense of higher in terms of physical elevation, we can understand God's dwelling place as a higher plane of existence, a higher dimension of reality. Brought into modern scientific terms, physicists speculate that there are *at least* seven more dimensions than the we experience (height, depth, length).

I don't profess to understand this myself, but in hypothesizing a ten-dimensional universe, it seems that modern science is only now beginning to catch up to the realities of God revealed in ancient Scripture. Within the pages we see fantastic ideas of angels, chariots of fire, heavenly visions, and, most profoundly, the physically resurrected Jesus moving in and out of the visible sight of his disciples. We are also told that we are surrounded by a great cloud of witnesses—those who have gone on before us and continue to cheer us on in our earthly race.

It's from this place, then, that Christ returns to sit in final judgment of all; those alive at the time of his return to our earthly plain as well as those who have already died in their mortal bodies. This second coming into our world will not be like the first. In the first appearance, Jesus came in weakness and humility to identify with our weakness and shame. However, as the triumphant, victorious, resurrected King of all Creation, Christ's second coming will be one of power and command. It will not be a little recognized event but will be unmistakable to everyone on the Earth. Jesus himself tells his disciples:

And then the sign of the Son of Man will appear in the sky, and then all the tribes of the earth will mourn, and they will see the Son of Man coming on the clouds of the sky with power and great glory. (Matthew 24:30)

The Apostle Paul also writes in 1 Thessalonians 4:16-17:

For the Lord Himself will descend from heaven with a shout, with the voice of the archangel and with the trumpet of God, and the dead in Christ will rise first. Then we who are alive and remain will be caught up in the air, and so we shall always be with the Lord.

Paul's language here is not only meant to address the Thessalonians' concern that somehow the Resurrection had already happened and that they or their dead loved ones had missed it but also to describe the return of Christ in the familiar image of a victorious king returning from conquest. Far from depicting a secret return, this passage is written to dispel the fears that would naturally accompany such an event. The return of a king to his walled city from the victory of battle would have been announced loudly by trumpet and fanfare. The people, hearing the approach of the king, would fling wide their doors, rush out to meet their heroic savior, and parade him back into the city for celebration and rejoicing.

Paul takes great care to assure the Thessalonians of two things: first, when Christ returns, it will not be in secret, but it will be known by all. And, second, when Christ returns, the resurrection will call forth first the bodies of those already dead and present in spirit with the Lord as he returns, and then those living will be transformed. And this will all happen in one unified event as Christ brings Heaven and the Earth back together as one unified reality.

At the same time, Jesus teaches in John 5 that he will then sit in judgment over all people throughout history.

For not even the Father judges anyone, but He has given all judgment to the Son, so that all will honor the Son even as they honor the Father. He who does not honor the Son does not honor the Father who sent Him. Truly, truly, I say to you, he who hears My word, and believes Him who sent Me, has eternal life, and does not come into judgment, but has passed out of death into life. Truly, truly, I say to you, an hour is coming and now is, when the dead will hear the voice of the Son of God, and those who hear will live. For just as the Father has life in Himself, even so He gave the Son also to have life in Himself; and He gave Him authority to execute judgment because He is the Son of Man.

John 5:22-27

Paul likewise teaches of Christ's role as judge:

I solemnly charge you in the presence of God and of Christ Jesus, who is to judge the living and the dead, and by His appearing and His kingdom.

2 Timothy 4:1

We may not like the idea of a final judgment taking place, which once and for all sets all people either on the right hand of God or banishes them from his presence. However, not only is such a judgment the only way to demonstrate God's steadfast mercy and grace, but it is also clearly taught in Scripture.

For no man can lay a foundation other than the one which is laid, which is Jesus Christ. Now if any man builds on the foundation with gold, silver, precious stones, wood, hay, straw, each man's work will become evident; for the day will show it because it is to be revealed with fire, and the fire itself will test the quality of each man's work. If any man's work which he has built on it remains, he will receive a reward. If any man's work is burned up, he will suffer loss; but he himself will be saved, yet so as through fire. Do you not know that you are a temple of God and that the Spirit of God dwells in you? If any man destroys the temple of God, God will destroy him, for the temple of God is holy, and that is what you are."

1 Corinthians 3:11-17

And again:

For after all it is only just for God to repay with affliction those who afflict you, and to give relief to you who are afflicted and to us as well when the Lord Jesus will be revealed from heaven with His mighty angels in flaming fire, dealing out retribution to those who do not know God and to those who do not obey the gospel of our Lord Jesus. These will pay the penalty of eternal destruction, away from the presence of the Lord and from the glory of His power, when He comes to be glorified in His saints on that day, and to be marveled at among all who have believed—for our testimony to you was believed.

2 Thessalonians 1:6-10

Consider the judge who sees the guilt of those who oppress and take advantage of the weak and vulnerable yet refuses to execute justice. Make no mistake: God is patient and gracious. It is His grace and mercy that have delayed the judgment for so long, giving all people the opportunity to repent and receive the forgiveness made available in Jesus Christ. But those who steadfastly refuse to accept this offer of pardon must one day stand on their own righteousness to defend their transgressions. And Scripture is clear what the outcome of this approach will be.

The Resurrection of the Body

The Christian faith is fundamentally one of incarnation. From the very first words of the Bible, it is made clear that God values the physical world He has created, and although it is utterly and entirely corrupted by sin, He doesn't abandon it to its fate. Instead, God immediately sets about redeeming, restoring, and reconciling what was lost. The curse of sin spoken over Adam, Eve, the serpent, and the earth in Genesis 3 is merely a statement of facts.

God's first act in response to this new reality is to make a covering for Adam and Eve with the skin of an animal. God's concern for them included and prioritized their physical well-being. Addressing that well-being came at the cost of a life. The spilling of blood was necessary to atone for what had been done, and in so doing, God covered their shame and protected their bodies from the harshness of the world–like the thorns that would infest the ground.

God's promise to Abraham included the land of Canaan, a physical home for his descendants to reside. In the Law He gave through Moses, God made provision for those with no other physical place to reside or gain sustenance by prohibiting the Israelites from harvesting from the borders of their fields. This would leave some minimal amount of food available to those who had no household to which they belonged: the widow, orphan, and foreigner traveling through the land. It was a way of providing for those literally on the margins, and the contrast this presented to the other cultures surrounding God's people was intended as a witness to a God who cares and provides for each and every need.

God's plan of redemption ultimately came about in the incarnation of Jesus Christ through the lineage of the family of Abraham. Jesus didn't appear through an interdimensional portal. He didn't spring forth from the ground, sky, sacred oak, or any other mythical means. Yes, he was born of a virgin, but in this, he was obtaining from humanity a true human nature and body. In other words, Jesus was not a simulation or imitation of a human being. He was truly human and, as we have already discussed, truly God.

Why would God ordain the redemption of the world in this manner? Even more than that, why would God ordain the redemption of the world at all? The witness of the whole of Scripture inevitably points to the fact that when He said that all the things He had created were "good," or in the Hebrew, *tov*, God meant it.

So then, why would it be that the ultimate hope given by God's plan of redemption, restoration, and reconciliation be anything other than the complete physical resurrection of all things? Why would we ever look to a disembodied existence floating around on clouds somewhere as the final word of the good news of our salvation through Jesus Christ? The answer is simply that this is the sinful imagination of fallen humanity as demonstrated time and again in countless religions, from Gnostic cults to Eastern religions such as Buddhism and Hinduism to even more recent Western philosophies such as transcendentalism and existentialism. These philosophies separate the physical from the spiritual, giving primacy to the spiritual. However, the early Christians and the apostles strongly opposed such interpretations of Christ's Kingdom and gospel. The Apostle John wrote in his second epistle:

> *For many deceivers has gone out into the world, those who do not acknowledge Jesus Christ as coming in the flesh. This is the deceiver and the antichrist.*

> 2 John 1:7

And Paul writes in his first letter to the Corinthians:

> *For if the dead are not raised, not even Christ has been raised; and if Christ has not been raised, your faith is worthless; you are still in your sins. Then those also who have fallen asleep in Christ have perished. If we have hoped in Christ in this life only, we are of all men most to be pitied. But now Christ has been raised from the dead, the first fruits of those who are asleep.*

> 1 Corinthians 15:16-20

The promise of resurrection is proclaimed throughout the New Testament as the ultimate hope of our salvation. As Romans 8 states in the opening of this chapter, the whole of creation waits in anticipation for that day because it too has been subjected to the burden of sin as a consequence of human rebellion.

But this worldview isn't limited to the New Testament. Just as God's act in Genesis 3 to cover Adam and Eve's nakedness; His covenant promise to Abram in Genesis 15; His provision of the ram to take the place of Isaac as the sacrifice in Genesis 22; the sacrificial system of the Levitical law; and the many other passages throughout the Old Testament point to the full revelation of God's plan in Christ, so too do God's promises to the people and the prophetic visions of Isaiah and, most especially, Ezekiel's Valley of Dry Bones point to the promise of resurrection.

Perhaps most poignant is the parallel between Genesis 2 and Revelation 21-22, a story that begins in a garden and ends in a garden city. God and man walk and talk together in Eden, and once again, in the end, Heaven and Earth rejoin one another. With sin once and for all expunged from this physical plane, the higher dimension of God's space can welcome us back without destruction.

So much of popular Christianity over the last 200 years has misunderstood and misrepresented how this story ends, and this, I believe, is the design of the enemy. By obscuring where we are going, he can more effectively mislead us. Reclaiming the ancient and original understanding of the final chapters of our world's narrative from novel and spurious nineteenth-century corruption is critical for effective Christian living and to restore true hope to many who desire Christ. However, that would require further in-depth study. For now, let's simply state that Heaven is great, but it's not the *end* of the world. There is an even greater hope promised by the Word of God than going to Heaven when we die, and that is, ultimately, Heaven and Earth are once again coming together.

The pressure to adopt a divided view of ourselves and our world as one where spiritual and physical realities have no bearing on one another must be resisted. This is not only a view shaped by pagan worldviews like Platonism, but it also has grave consequences for our lives. The most obvious is neglect for the everyday things God Himself has shown us He values, like provision for the poor, the marginalized, and the neglected. However, less obvious is how adopting such a divided worldview tacitly endorses ideas such as "My body, my choice" or that one's true identity is found within and has nothing to do with one's physical body or DNA. The explosion in gender dysmorphia may well be linked to the prevalence of evangelical Christianity's embrace of a Neoplatonic view of the body and the physical world over the last century. In this world, the physical is devalued, and only a heavenly existence is seen as authentic and genuine.

The Life Everlasting

The resurrection of all people is a prerequisite for the judgement over which Christ will preside. Both those who died in Christ and those not in Christ will be resurrected to face this final judgment. Continuing from John 5 above, Jesus says:

> *Do not marvel at this; for an hour is coming, in which all who are in the tombs will hear His voice, and will come forth; those who did the good deeds to a resurrection of life, those who committed the evil deeds to a resurrection of judgment.*

John 5:28-29

Two different fates await these two groups. There is much disagreement on what exactly the judgment is that awaits those who are not found to be in Christ. The descriptions in Scripture range from a lake of fire to outer darkness to being forced to kneel and worship in the holy presence of God, even in His very throne room. There are some obvious contradictions if any of these are taken too literally.

What we can say with absolute certainty is that it is not an experience anyone would desire. There are also different views on whether the torment of judgment is eternal or if the ultimate punishment is being destroyed and ceasing to be.

Both camps cite Sscriptures to support their positions. But for our purposes here, our focus is not on those who reject God's offer of redemption, restoration, and reconciliation. Our confession is regarding us who believe in the name of Jesus. As for the other, we'd do well to heed Christ's words to Peter regarding John's destiny in John 21:22: "If I want him to remain until I come, what is that to you? You follow me!" In other words, let's let God be God and not meddle in His business.

For those of us who believe in Christ and are raised to eternal life, we have already seen through other Scriptures cited here that this means eternally existing in the presence of God. It is a physical resurrection but one in a world where God is no longer distant. We see him face to face. Revelation 21 and 22 describe a world where there is no more pain, no more sadness, and where God Himself lives with us. He is the very light, and there is no longer any need for the sun. He is the source of our life, all that sustains us and feeds us.

When Jesus says in John 14:6, "I am the way, the truth, and the life," he is not only giving gospel instructions, but also pointing ahead to the new reality; the reality that was already breaking through at the time he spoke those words. He, Jesus Christ, is the *telos*, that from which all things have come and to which all things are going. He *is* life. He *is* truth. And he *is* the only way by which we can receive either.

Discussion Questions

1. How does the word *telos* inform your view of Christ, the Gospel, and the Christian life?

   _____

   _____

   _____

   _____

   _____

2. What implications does Christ's ascension to the right hand of the Father and his ruling and reigning there forever have for his second coming? What implications does this have for his authority to execute judgment?

   _____

   _____

   _____

   _____

3. How does God's judgment also embody His mercy? Why might His judgment and mercy joined together be important?

   _____

   _____

   _____

   _____

   _____

4. How does the ultimate hope of resurrection influence your attitudes toward daily living? How might the idea of an only spiritual eternity subtly have crept into your thoughts about the Christian hope? How might realizing the Bible teaches a fully embodied eternal life change those thoughts?

    _____

    _____

    _____

    _____

    _____

5. Does the assurance of all the promise of God, clearly and systematically outlined in the Apostles' Creed bring you to a place of confidence, hope, and victory? What would living that out look like?

    _____

    _____

    _____

    _____

    _____

6. For further reading on the topic of our ultimate hope, I highly recommend the book *Surprised by Hope: Rethinking Heaven, the Resurrection, and the Mission of the Church*, by N.T. Wright, Harper One Publishing, 2008.

    _____

    _____

    _____

SCAN HERE to learn more about
Invite Ministries—created to invite people to a deeper
faith and living relationship with Jesus Christ

www.ingramcontent.com/pod-product-compliance
Lightning Source LLC
Chambersburg PA
CBHW020424130626
46549CB00006B/2723